THE
STRATEGIST

THE
STRATEGIST

BE THE LEADER
YOUR BUSINESS NEEDS

CYNTHIA A. MONTGOMERY
HARVARD BUSINESS SCHOOL

Collins

First published in 2012 by Collins

HarperCollins*Publishers*
77–85 Fulham Palace Road
London W6 8JB

www.harpercollins.co.uk

10 9 8 7 6 5 4 3 2 1

Text © Cynthia Montgomery 2012

The author asserts her moral right to be identified as the author of this work.

A catalogue record for this book is available from the British Library.

HB ISBN: 978-0-00-742667-6
TPB ISBN: 978-0-00742668-3

Printed and bound in Great Britain by Clays Ltd, St Ives plc.

MIX
Paper from
responsible sources
FSC **FSC™ C007454**
www.fsc.org

FSC™ is a non-profit international organisation established to promote the responsible management of the world's forests. Products carrying the FSC label are independently certified to assure consumers that they come from forests that are managed to meet the social, economic and ecological needs of present and future generations, and other controlled sources.

Find out more about HarperCollins and the environment at
www.harpercollins.co.uk/green

TO

ANNEKE, MATHEA, AND NILS

THAT YOU MAY FIND PLACES WHERE YOU CAN MAKE A DIFFERENCE THAT MATTERS

AND TO BJØRN, FOREVERMORE

ACKNOWLEDGMENTS

A CLOSING LINE FROM *Huckleberry Finn* often came to mind as I worked on this manuscript: "If I'd a knowed what a trouble it was to make a book I wouldn't a tackled it." Looking back on the process from this side of the finish line, I'm more impressed by the communal aspect of the project, and the good people it has brought my way.

I am grateful for financial support from the Division of Research at Harvard Business School, and for permission from *Harvard Business Review* to use parts of an article I had previously published there. I am grateful, too, for the opportunity to work with Lynda Applegate, Jackie Baugher, and Kathleen Mara in Executive Education; Cathyjean Gustafson in Morgan Hall; Imelda Dundas in Faculty Development; and Chris Allen and others at the Baker Library. One of my most rewarding collaborations was with Sharon Johnson and David Kiron as we batted around early ideas for the book.

My colleague David Yoffie's cases on Gucci and Apple are mainstays in my executive education courses and jumping off points for two chapters in this book. More generally, the intellectual community at HBS and in particular in the Strategy group has had an enormous influence on how I see the world and what I teach.

Once the book was under way, a whole new community emerged: Jim Levine, who showed me the many ways good literary agencies create value; my editor at HarperCollins, Hollis Heimbouch, whose judgment I counted on; Charles Burke, whose adept way with words bettered many rough paragraphs; and Karen Blumenthal, Kent Lineback, Susanna Margolis, and Lisa Baker who helped with various drafts of the proposal and manuscript.

It has been a privilege to work with the business owners and managers from around the world who inspired this book and made me see how much they as strategists add to their businesses. I thank them for sharing their stories and encouraging me to share mine.

On the home front, I thank my husband, Birger, who kept the candles burning when the lights went out.

IN THE END, IT IS IMPORTANT TO REMEMBER THAT WE CANNOT BECOME WHAT WE NEED TO BE BY REMAINING WHAT WE ARE.

MAX DE PREE, CEO OF HERMAN MILLER, IN *LEADERSHIP IS AN ART*

CONTENTS

THE
STRATEGIST

WHAT I LEARNED IN OFFICE HOURS

Terenure Branch Tel. 4907035

YOU'RE ABOUT TO get a revisionist view of strategy. It's not that what you've learned is incorrect. It's that it's incomplete.

Strategy is a fundamental course at nearly every business school in the world. I have been privileged to teach variations of it for more than thirty years—first at the University of Michigan, then at the Kellogg School at Northwestern, and for the last twenty-plus years at the Harvard Business School.

For most of that time I worked with MBA students, until the center of my teaching shifted to executive education. It was this experience, particularly a five-year stint in Harvard's Entrepreneur, Owner, President program (EOP), that inspired this book.[1] Working intimately with leaders from nearly every industry and nation as they confronted their own real-world strategic issues changed not only how I teach strategy, but, more fundamentally, how I think about it. The experience led me to challenge some of strategy's basic precepts, and ultimately to question both the culture and mind-set that have grown up around it. Even more important, teaching in EOP forced me to confront how strategy is really made in most businesses, and by whom.

All of this convinced me that it is time for a change. Time to approach strategy in a different way and time to transform the process from a mechanical, analytical activity to something deeper, more meaningful, and far more rewarding for a leader.

THE ROAD TO HERE

Fifty years ago strategy was taught as part of the general management curriculum in most business schools. In the academy as well as in practice, it was identified as the most important duty of the president— the person with overarching responsibility for setting a company's course and seeing the journey through. This vital role encompassed both formulation and implementation: thinking and doing combined.

Although strategy had considerable depth then, it didn't have much rigor. Heuristically, managers used the ubiquitous SWOT model (Strengths, Weaknesses, Opportunities, and Threats) to assess their businesses and identify attractive competitive positions. How best to do that, though, was far from clear. Other than making lists of various factors to consider, managers had few tools to help them make these judgments.

In the 1980s and '90s, my colleague Michael E. Porter broke important new ground in the field. His watershed came in firming up the Opportunities and Threats side of the analysis by bringing much-needed economic theory and empirical evidence to strategy's underpinnings, providing a far more sophisticated way to assess a firm's competitive environment. This led to a revolution in both the practice and teaching of strategy. In particular, managers came to understand the profound impact industry forces could have on the success of their businesses and how they could use that information to position their firms propitiously.

Advances over the next few decades not only refined the tools but spawned a whole new industry. Strategy in many ways became the bailiwick of specialists—legions of MBAs and strategy consultants, armed with frameworks, techniques, and data—eager to help managers analyze their industries or position their firms for strategic advantage. In truth, they had a lot to offer. My own academic training and research in this period reflected this intellectual environment, and what I did in the classroom for many years thereafter was a living embodiment of this "new" field of strategy.

In time, though, a host of unintended consequences developed from what in its own right was a very good thing. Most notably, strategy became more about formulation than implementation, and more about getting the analysis right at the outset than living with a strategy over time. Equally problematic, the leader's unique role as arbiter and steward of strategy had been eclipsed. While countless books have been written about strategy in the last thirty years, virtually nothing has been written about the *strategist* and what this vital role requires of the person who shoulders it.

It wasn't until years into this shift that I fully realized what had happened. It was classic Shakespeare: As a field, we had hoisted ourselves on our own petard. We had demoted strategy from the top of the organization to a specialist function. Chasing a new ideal, we had lost sight of the value of what we had—the richness of judgment, the continuity of purpose, the will to commit an organization to a particular path. With all good intentions, we had backed strategy into a narrow corner and reduced it to a left-brain exercise. In doing so, we lost much of its vitality and much of its connection to the day-to-day life of a company, and we lost sight of what it takes to lead the effort.

Teaching in the EOP program drove these insights home for me.

When I first started working with the group, I used a curriculum that was much like one I would use in any executive program. Through a series of class discussions and presentations, we discussed the enduring principles of strategy, the frameworks that capture them, and a series of case studies that brought the concepts and tensions alive. We still do that—and it's a valuable part of what we do.

But in between class sessions, the EOP students—all accomplished executives and entrepreneurs—started to ask if they could meet me in my office to talk about various situations they were facing in their companies. These conversations often took place at unusual hours, and sometimes lasted far into the evening. Most started out predictably enough: We talked about the conditions in their industries, the strengths and weaknesses of their own companies, and their efforts to build or extend a competitive advantage. Some discussions ended there, and a thoughtful application of whatever we'd been doing in class seemed to meet the need.

Often, though, these conversations took a different turn. Alongside all the conventional questions were ones about what to do when the limits of analysis had been reached and the way forward was still not clear; questions about when to move away from an existing competitive advantage and when to try to stay the course; questions about reinventing a business or identifying a new purpose, a new reason to matter. Even though many of the companies at issue were remarkably successful (one had grown from a start-up to $2 billion in revenue in just nine years), almost none had the kind of long-run sustainable competitive advantage that strategy books tout as the Holy Grail.

Working with these managers, typically over three years, and hearing the stories within the stories, I came to see that we cannot afford to think of strategy as something fixed, a problem that is solved and settled. Strategy—the system of value creation that underlies a company's competitive position and uniqueness—has to be embraced as something open, not something closed. It is a system that evolves, moves, and changes.

In these late-night one-on-one conversations, I also saw something else: I saw the strategist, the human being, the leader. I saw how responsible these executives feel for getting things right. I saw how invested they are in these choices, and how much is at stake. I saw the energy and commitment they bring to this endeavor. I saw their confidential concerns, too: "Am I doing this job well? Am I providing the leadership my company needs?"

And, more than anything, I saw in these conversations the tremendous potential these leaders hold in their hands, and the profound opportunity they have to make a difference in the life of a company. In those moments together, we both came to understand that if their businesses were going to pull away from the pack, to create a difference that mattered, it had to start with them.

A NEW UNDERSTANDING

In all our lives there are times of learning that transform us, that distance us from the familiar, and make us see it in new ways. For me, the EOP experience was one of those times. It not only changed some of my most central views about strategy; it gave me a new perspective on the strategist, and on the power and promise of that role.

In these pages I will share with you what I have learned. In doing so, I hope that you will gain a new understanding about what strategy is, why it matters, and what you must do to lead the effort. I also hope that you will come to see that beyond the analytics and insights of highly skilled advisors and the exhortations of "how-to" guides, there is a need for judgment, for continuity, for responsibility that rests squarely with you—as a leader.

Because this role rests with you, *The Strategist* is a personal call to action. It reinstates an essential component of the strategy-making process that has been ignored for decades: You. The leader. The person who must live the questions that matter most.

That's why my ultimate goal here is not to "teach strategy," but to equip and inspire you to be a strategist, a leader whose time at the helm could have a profound effect on the fortunes of your organization.

1

STRATEGY AND LEADERSHIP

Does your company matter?

That's the most important question every business leader must answer.

If you closed its doors today, would your customers suffer any real loss?[1] How long would it take, and how difficult would it be, for them to find another firm that could meet those needs as well as you did?

Most likely, you don't think about your company and what it does in quite this way. Even if you've hired strategy consultants, or spent weeks developing a strategic plan, the question probably still gives you pause.

If it does or if you're not sure how to respond, you're not alone.

I know this because I've spent the better part of my life working with leaders on their business strategies. Again and again, I've seen them struggle to explain why their companies truly matter. It's a difficult question.

Can you answer it?

If you cannot, or if you're uncertain of your answer, join me as I explore this question with a group of executives now gathering.

It is evening on the campus of the Harvard Business School. The kickoff orientation to the Entrepreneur, Owner, President program ("EOP" for short), one of the flagship executive programs at the school, is about to begin. Along with five of my fellow faculty, I sit in the "sky deck," the last and highest row of seats, in Aldrich 112, an amphitheater-style classroom characteristic of the school, and watch as the newest group of executives stream into the room.

I see that there are considerably more men than women, and that the majority appear to be in their late thirties to mid-forties. Most exude an air of seasoned self-confidence. That's no surprise—they're all owners, CEOs, or COOs of privately held companies with annual revenues of $10 million to $2 billion—the kind of small- to medium-size enterprises that drive much of the global economy. Most arrived on campus within the last few hours and have had just enough time to find their dorm rooms and meet the members of their living groups before heading here to Aldrich.

The information they provided in their applications tells part of their stories: Richard, a third-generation U.S. steel fabricator; Drazen, CEO of a media firm in Croatia; Anna, founder and head of one of the largest private equity groups in South America; and Praveen, the scion of a family conglomerate in India. But this is just a taste of their diversity and accomplishments. The richer details and the breadth of the class will emerge in the weeks ahead.

As the clock ticks past the hour, some last-minute arrivals burst through the door. They are typical first-time EOPers in their lack of concern about being late. Most of these people hail from worlds where meetings don't start until they arrive. That will change in the coming days, as they make the adjustment from the top-of-the-line leather chairs in their offices back home to the standard-issue seats that line the classrooms. Indeed, for their time here, they will be without many of the supports they rely on in their daily lives, such as administrative assistants and subordinates to whom they can delegate work and problems. Families are strongly discouraged from living near campus and are prohibited from dorms once classes begin. BlackBerrys and cell phones are allowed, but never in class.

A final hush settles as the program begins with an overview of who's here: 164 participants from thirty-five countries, with a collective 2,922 years of experience. Two-thirds of their businesses are in service industries, the remainder in manufacturing.

They are here to participate in an intensive management boot camp for experienced business leaders. It spans topics in finance, marketing, organizational behavior, accounting, negotiations, and strategy, and runs for nine weeks in total, divided into three three-week sessions spread over three years. Between sessions, students return to their businesses and start to apply what they have learned. Debriefs the following year are an opportunity for feedback and reflection on what has worked and what hasn't. This structure has given the faculty an exceptional opportunity to develop a hands-on curriculum that brings theory and practice much closer together, even for a school that has always championed the connection.

Why do these talented, seasoned managers from every major world culture come to this program? As heads of their companies, why do they elect to spend tens of thousands of dollars to send *themselves* to school?

THE VIEW FROM THE BALCONY

If past participants are any indication, these executives have not come to seek specific answers to narrow questions. They have come to learn how to be more effective leaders and to find ways to make their businesses more successful. Successful in what ways, and through what means, for most, is still an open question. They are here to throw themselves into the program, to be challenged, to discover what they might learn in this environment.

This experience will be an important juncture for many, in their careers and even their lives. What they learn here will lead them to think in broader, more far-reaching ways. To explain how this happens, I've always liked the metaphor of a dance taking place in a great hall. Most dancers spend all their time on the dance floor, moved by the music, jostled by dancers around them, completely absorbed in the flow. But it's not until they extricate themselves from the crowd and move to the balcony above that the larger picture becomes clear. It is then that overall patterns become apparent and new perspectives emerge. Often these reveal opportunities for better choices about what to do down on the dance floor.

Many EOPers have spent years without ever leaving the dance floor. Absorbed by the day-to-day challenges of running a business, they've never gone to the balcony. On one level, our job is to help them understand the value of going to the balcony in the first place. On another, it is to equip them with the tools to see their dances in new ways, ways that reveal options they may never have considered before.

THE STRATEGY COURSE

When it's time for the faculty to introduce their courses, I stand and give a quick summary of the work we'll be doing in strategy. Like most businesspeople, these managers are likely to be familiar with at least a vague definition of strategy. The word itself comes from the ancient Greek for "general"—specifically for the general on campaign in the field. In business, strategy is a company's campaign in the marketplace: the domain in which it competes, how it competes, and what it wants to accomplish.

We will begin our journey with the fundamentals—what strategy is, how to craft it, and how to evaluate it. We'll then push the envelope on current practice by challenging strategy's elusive goal—the long-run sustainable competitive advantage—and introduce a dynamic model of strategy that is better grounded and better suited for the competitive realities most managers face.

All of this material is prelude to the last and most challenging task they will face here, when every member of the class will be asked to apply the concepts and frameworks we've been studying to their own companies and present their own strategies for critiquing by their EOP colleagues. The exercise takes many days and, in the end, the class votes on a winner, what they consider the "best strategy" in the group.

This step from the general to the highly particular, from the objective to the subjective, is where things become profoundly real for most executives. This is when the appraisals of cases—now *their* cases—get deadly serious and the discussions especially heartfelt. These are competitive people. A spirit of intense rivalry prevails. Most refine their strategies through multiple iterations, often working through the night for one more iteration. These weeks are arduous for some, exhilarating for others, and, for most, a healthy mix of both.

GETTING TO THE REALITY OF YOUR STRATEGY

Having seen hundreds if not thousands of such strategies in their initial form, what is clear to me is this: Many leaders haven't thought about their own strategies in a very deep way. Often, there is a curious gap between their intellectual understanding of strategy and their ability to drive those insights home in their own businesses.

Some EOPers find it extremely difficult to identify why their companies exist. Accustomed to describing their businesses by the industries they're in or the products they make, they can't articulate the specific needs their businesses fill, or the unique points that distinguish them from competitors on anything beyond a superficial level. Nor have they spent much time thinking concretely about where they want their companies to be in ten years and the forces, internal and external, that will get them there.

If leaders aren't clear about this, imagine the confusion in their businesses three or four levels lower. Yet, people throughout a business—in marketing, production, service, as well as near the top of the organization—must make decisions every day that could and should be based on some shared sense of what the company is trying to be and do. If they disagree about that, or simply don't understand it, how can they make consistent decisions that move the company forward? Similarly, how can leaders expect customers, providers of capital, or other stakeholders to understand what is really important about their companies if they themselves can't identify it? This is truly basic—there is no way a business can thrive until these questions are answered.

Even so, the exercises in EOP are designed to do more than set high standards, communicate concepts, and improve participants' existing strategies. The overarching goal is something different, something deeper and more personal. It is to make clear to these executives that strategy is the heart of the ongoing leadership their companies need from them. That's why competition for "best strategy" is so hard fought and generates so much energy. CEOs, accustomed to asking questions and being deferred to, are challenged by their peers and encouraged to think and rethink parts of their strategies they'd taken for granted. Most of them describe it as a pivotal experience that fundamentally changes their views of their own businesses.

Behind the scenes, though, the real contest is closer in: It's each of these leaders pushing their own ideas to the increasingly high standards they themselves have come to demand of excellent strategies and of themselves as leaders. It's that process, more than any short-term answers they might find here, that will serve them well in the long run.

LEADERSHIP AND STRATEGY ARE INSEPARABLE

Many leaders today do not understand the ongoing, intimate connection between leadership and strategy. These two aspects of what leaders do, once tightly linked, have grown apart. Now specialists help managers analyze their industries and position their businesses for competitive advantage, and strategy has become largely a job for experts, or something confined to an annual planning process. In this view, once a strategy has been identified, and the next steps specified, the job of the strategist is finished. All that remains to be done is to implement the plan and defend the sustainable competitive advantage it has wrought. Or at least that's the positive take on the story.

But, if this were so, the process of crafting a strategy would be easy to separate from the day-to-day management of a firm. All a leader would have to do is figure it out once, or hire a consulting firm to figure it out, and make sure it's brilliant. If this were so, the strategist wouldn't have to be concerned with how the organization gets from here to there—the great execution challenge—or how it will capitalize on the learning it accumulates along the way.

But this is not so.

What's been forgotten is that strategy is not a destination or a solution. It's not a problem to be solved and settled. It's a journey. It needs continuous, not intermittent, leadership.

It needs a strategist.

Good strategies are never frozen—signed, sealed, and delivered. No matter how carefully conceived, or how well implemented, any strategy put into place in a company today will eventually fail if leaders see it as a finished product. There will always be aspects of the plan that need to be clarified. There will always be countless contingencies, good and bad, that could not have been fully anticipated. There will always be opportunities to capitalize on the learning a business has accumulated along the way.

The strategist is the one who must shepherd this ongoing process, who must stand watch, identify and weigh, decide and move, time and time again. The strategist is the one who must decline certain opportunities and pursue others. Consultants' expertise and considered judgments can help, as can perspectives and information from people throughout an organization. But, in the end, it is the strategist who bears the responsibility for setting a firm's course and making the choices day after day that continuously refine that course.

That is why strategy and leadership must be reunited at the highest level of an organization. All leaders—not just those who are here tonight—must accept and own strategy as the heart of their responsibilities.

I say little of this tonight in the classroom. But it is on my mind as I

return to my seat in the sky deck and reflect on all the would-be strategists I've worked with over the years as well as those of you who are just
starting out. My hope is that you will come not only to understand the
vital role of the strategist, but also to embrace it for yourself.

Five years ago, when I first started teaching in EOP, I heard the
program described as challenging and transformative. At the time,
"challenging" struck me as right, but "transformative" seemed closer to
hype. Having seen it happen again and again, I now share the optimism.

As our orientation session draws to a close, I join the executives and
fellow faculty as we head en masse to Kresge Hall for cocktails and din-
ner. Our work is about to begin in earnest.

> In all my classes, I pose one fundamental question: "Are you a
> strategist?" Sometimes it's spoken, often it's only implicit, but it's
> always there. We talk about the questions strategists ask, about how
> strategists think, about what strategists do. My intent is not to coach
> these executives in strategy in the way they might learn finance
> or marketing. As business heads, they aren't going to be functional
> specialists. But they do need to be strategists.
>
> Are you a strategist?
>
> It's a question all business leaders must answer because strategy
> is so bedrock crucial to every company. No matter how hard you and
> your people work, no matter how wonderful your culture, no matter
> how good your products, or how noble your motives, if you don't get
> strategy right, everything else you do is at risk.
>
> My goal in this book is to help you develop the skills and
> sensibilities this role demands, and to encourage you to answer the
> question for yourself. It's a difficult role and it may be tempting to
> try to sidestep it. It requires a level of courage and openness to ask
> the fundamental questions about your company and to live with
> those questions day after day. But little you do as a leader is likely to
> matter more.

2

ARE YOU A STRATEGIST?

HERE'S A TEST of your strategic thinking. It's the same one I give my EOPers right at the beginning of the course.

Step into the shoes of Richard Manoogian, CEO of Masco Corporation, a highly successful company on the verge of a momentous decision.[1] You've got a big pile of money and must decide whether to invest it in a far-reaching new business venture. The stakes are high, and it's not an easy or obvious decision. If you don't go ahead, you could be passing up an opportunity for growth in a new direction and hundreds of millions of dollars in future profits. If you take the plunge and turn out to be wrong, you may have wasted $1–2 billion. Either way, you will have to live with the results for many years.

To make the decision, you'll first need to know something about Masco and its marketplace. The story begins more than two decades ago, but its lessons are timeless, and the intervening years allow us to take a long view on the company and the industry.

FIRST, CONSIDER THE COMPANY

It's 1986. Masco is a successful $1.15 billion company that has just recorded its twenty-ninth consecutive year of earnings growth. Its ability to wring outsized profits out of industries that are neither high tech nor glamorous has won it the monicker of "Master of the Mundane" on Wall Street. Its portfolio includes faucets, kitchen and bathroom cabinets, locks and building hardware, and a variety of other household products.[2] Masco expects the businesses to generate $2 billion in free cash flow over the next few years.

What would you do with all that money? Masco's leaders want to tackle other mundane businesses where their prowess can "change the game." They envision becoming the "Procter & Gamble of consumer durables." In their immediate sights is the U.S. household furniture business, where they see another opportunity to seize profitable dominance of a sleepy industry.

Is Manoogian's idea a promising one? If so, is Masco the company to lead the charge?

When I raise these questions the first morning in class, the executives don't immediately jump up. Like you, they enjoy being the decision maker; it's the role they play in their real-life jobs, but they're reluctant to put themselves on the line with a group they've just met. With some coaxing, though, we're soon deep into Masco's situation and the issues Manoogian faces.

The case for Manoogian's strategy looks compelling. Through a long record of triumphs in durable goods industries, Masco distinguished itself through efficient manufacturing, good management, and innovation. Its biggest success to date was reinventing the faucet business. Prior to Masco's entry, the industry was highly fragmented and had a general lack of brand recognition, minimal advertising, and a low level of salesperson training. Leveraging the company's deep metalworking expertise, garnered in its early years as a supplier to the automotive industry, Masco's founder, Richard's father Alex, solved an engineering problem

that made one-handle faucets workable. When he couldn't interest fau
cet companies in his patented innovation, Masco began making and
selling the faucets itself.

Homeowners loved them, finding them a big improvement over traditional faucets that forced users to fiddle with hot and cold water sepa-
rately. This extra functionality was particularly valued in kitchens where
utility and maintenance-free operation were important. Not neglecting
two-handle faucets, the company introduced a model with a new type of
valve. This design, also patented, eliminated rubber washers, the major
cause of faucet failure.

Masco went on to innovate in many other aspects of these new
products, from basic manufacturing to distribution and marketing. It
was the first to create brand recognition for a faucet with its Delta and
Peerless brands. It was the first to introduce see-through packaging, to
market faucets direct to the consumer through the do-it-yourself chan-
nel, and to advertise faucets on TV during the Olympics. In refashioning an industry of "me-too" products and boldly setting itself apart
from others, Masco demonstrated that it was creative, able to apply traditional capabilities in new ways, and willing to take risks and make
them pay off—abilities Richard Manoogian hoped would enable him to
transform the furniture business.

NOW CONSIDER THE INDUSTRY

At the time Manoogian was weighing this decision, household furniture was a $14 billion business in the United States that didn't make
much money. With high transportation costs, low productivity, and
eroding prices, it had about 2 percent annual growth, and return on
sales, on average, was about 4 percent. There were more than 2,500
manufacturers, but 80 percent of sales came from only four hundred.
Not all players were small, but most were, and many were family firms
that had stuck it out through thick and thin, reluctant to leave the only
livelihood their families had known for generations. Making matters

worse, both sales and profits were cyclical and tied to broad economic factors such as new home starts and sales of existing homes.

Management in the industry was generally regarded as unsophisticated, and hadn't made many significant changes in the previous fifty years. Wesley Collins, a furniture executive and trenchant observer of industry conditions, summed it up dramatically:

> *When everything else in our lives was changing, furniture stood its ground. While we put a man on the moon . . . furniture put another steak on the backyard grill and muttered, "My god, the price of oak went up again."*
>
> *When videotape put the home movie camera in the trash can forever, and tape cassettes put the plastic record-maker six feet under, and word processors put typewriters in the closet, and microwave popcorn killed the makers of popcorn makers . . . the furniture industry said, "Thanks, but we'll stand pat."*
>
> *While we sat on our tuffets, the consumer forgot all about us. Our share of consumer expenditures slipped year after year. We lost over 40 percent of the retail furniture space in America, 25 percent of the retailers shut their doors, and department stores discontinued furniture right and left for products that gave them a better ratio of margin and turns per square foot.[3]*

Collins went on to say that "the average tobacco chewer spends more for Levi Garrett Chewing Tobacco every year than he does for furniture."

Most furniture purchases were discretionary and highly postponable, and, as Collins noted, there were many substitutes and lots of competition for the customer's dollar. New innovations and designs were quickly knocked off by competitors, eliminating any advantage the innovators might have momentarily enjoyed.

Equally distressing, in the United States, there was little brand recognition in the industry. Customers didn't know much about furniture and weren't motivated enough to find out. There was little advertising and consumer research had shown that many American adults could not name a single furniture brand. Think for a minute: "What brand of sofa do you have in your living room?" When I pick an executive in the class at random and ask this question, the response is usually a startled look, a long moment of silence, and then, something like "Brown leather?" Everyone laughs, but when I open the question to the entire class, only a few hands go up and they're inevitably executives from Europe. Yet when I ask how many of them know the brand of car their neighbors drive, virtually all hands go up. Yours probably would, too.

On top of its marketing challenges, the industry was riddled with inefficiencies, extreme product variety, and long lead times that frustrated customers. Buyers often received partial shipments; for example, a dining table might arrive weeks or months before the chairs that went with it.

The real issue, though, is not whether there are problems in the industry but what they mean. Are all these problems an opportunity for a courageous company with the right skills? Or are they red flags warning outsiders to stay away?

When I ask my executives whether they would take the plunge, most respond with a resounding "Yes!" They're energized, not intimidated, by the challenges. Most say, in effect, "Where there's challenge, there's opportunity." If it were an easy business, they say, some company would already have seized the opportunity: It would be much tougher to dislodge a strong leader than to gain ground in an industry like this where there are no big players, no Microsofts already established. "It's a horse race," someone once said, "and all the other horses are slow."

Further, they note, the furniture industry is much like the faucet industry before Masco entered. The opportunity is a great fit with Masco's manufacturing skills, its marketing savvy, and its strong management capabilities. It's another chance for Masco to bring money, sophistication, and discipline to a fragmented, unsophisticated, and chaotic industry.

Opponents can't get past how awful the furniture business is. They can't imagine any company overcoming such huge hurdles. So the arguments go back and forth. Enthusiasm and a gung-ho spirit on one side struggle against caution and concern on the other. In one discussion, an exasperated proponent blurted out, "Look, this isn't about being passive investors in some yet-to-be-invented furniture industry index fund. We're going to be players in this game. We can make things happen. If Starbucks or Under Armour had listened to you naysayers, they wouldn't have done anything!"

What's your inclination at this point?

Usually when the time comes for a decision in my classes, "Do it" wins definitively, by at least a 2-to-1 margin.

So what, in fact, happened?

Masco did enter and in a bold way. Over two years, it bought Henredon (high-end furniture) for $300 million, Drexel Heritage (mid-price) for $275 million, and Lexington Furniture (low–middle) for $250 million. Combined, the revenues from the three made Masco the second-largest player in the U.S. furniture industry. It followed up by spending $500 million for Universal Furniture Limited (low end), which had manufacturing operations in ten countries on three continents and followed a ready-to-assemble concept—component parts were manufactured in low-cost countries and shipped in containers to five U.S. locations for assembly. Now Masco was both the largest furniture company in the world and one of the only firms with products spanning nearly every price point, a strategy that had worked well for the firm in faucets.

In total, Masco spent $1.5 billion acquiring ten companies and another $250 million upgrading their manufacturing facilities and investing in new marketing programs.

Presenting Manoogian with its Gold Award in the Building Materials Industry, the *Wall Street Transcript* cited his

imagination, foresight and strategic sense. . . . Manoogian
has acquired low growth, mature products and become the
dominant player in those product categories. . . . [H]is most
recent set of acquisitions has been in the furniture industry. His
strategy is to do to the furniture industry what he did to the faucet
and kitchen cabinet industry. . . .[4]

With this historical update, the classroom crackles with energy. Executives who had advocated for bold action nod their heads to one another or give each other high-fives and thumbs-up, pleased that they've nailed their first Harvard case. I hear little "told-you-so" comments directed at the naysayers, who sit in grim silence. Someone once even called across the room: "Don't worry, Bob. One bad decision won't ruin your reputation. We won't hold it against you the rest of the program."

But it doesn't take long for those who opposed entry to speak up.

"But how did Masco do?"

"They bought great brand names," says someone.

"But how did they do?"

"They're number one in market share. What more do you want?"

"But did they make money?"

There, as it's said, is the rub.

When I post Masco's financial results, silence falls as people absorb the numbers. In a few seconds, there are whispered expletives around the room.

After thirty-two years of consecutive earnings growth, Masco's net income fell 30 percent. Two years later, operating earnings from furniture came to $80 million on sales of $1.4 billion, an operating margin of 6 percent, versus 14 percent for the rest of the company. After many years of struggle, Masco announced its intentions to sell its furniture businesses, leading one analyst to comment:

In the spring, management will go on the road with restated
financials illustrating their "core" earnings growth as if they
never entered the furniture business. They hope to rebuild investor
confidence in the old [pre-furniture] Masco . . . as a growth
company by showing their track record and prospects in the building
materials arena. Given the $2 billion furniture "mistake," this
won't be easy.

In a sad postscript, Masco discovered that exiting the furniture business was much harder than entering it. After a number of deals fell through, it eventually succeeded in selling its furniture firms, at a loss of some $650 million.[5] When it was all over, CEO Manoogian admitted, "The decision to go into the home furnishings business was probably one of the worst decisions I've made in 35 years."[6]

It's a sobering moment in the classroom. The executives there didn't intend to open their careers at the Harvard Business School by losing hundreds of millions of dollars their first morning.

So, let me ask you again, as I do the managers in my class: "Are you the strategist your business needs?"

3

THE MYTH OF THE SUPER-MANAGER

A S A STRATEGIST, what can you learn from Masco's foray into furniture and the support most executives give that ill-fated decision?

Even if you were undecided or skeptical about the furniture industry, I'm willing to bet that some part of you supported Masco's move. No one respects timid, passive managers. Bold, visionary leaders who have the confidence to take their firms in exciting new directions are widely admired. Isn't that a key part of strategy and leadership?

In truth, it is. But the confidence every good strategist needs can readily balloon into overconfidence. A belief that is unspoken but implied in much management thinking and writing today is that a highly competent manager can produce success in virtually any situation. One writer calls this "the sense of omnipotence that plagues American management, the belief that no event or situation is too complex or too unpredictable to be brought under management control."[1]

I call this belief, when taken to its extreme, the myth of the super-manager. It seems to come naturally to many successful entrepreneurs and senior managers who see themselves as action-oriented problem solvers, confident doers for whom difficulties are daunting but solvable challenges. I see it behind Masco's leap into furniture manufacturing and behind executives' choice of the same path every time I teach the case. Confidence matters. But there's much more to strategy and leadership than a steadfast belief that a daring vision backed by good management can overcome virtually all obstacles. Without the rest of it, "bold" too often becomes "reckless."

Look at what such thinking did to Masco. Operating profitability dropped to half its historical average, and the firm's stock price was lower when it left the furniture industry than when it entered ten years earlier. And money was only part of the cost. Where Wall Street had spoken of Masco as a "Master of the Mundane," it began to speak of the company's "past glory" and "bitter shareholders."[2] The company lost momentum as its leaders spent years distracted by a massive venture that ultimately failed.

For Masco, its move into furniture was a defining moment, but not a positive one. A legacy built over decades was shattered, an affirmation of a well-known Warren Buffett maxim: "It takes twenty years to build a reputation and five minutes to ruin it." All because the strategist got this one choice wrong.

What happened?

Your instinct, like most managers', is probably to seek the answer by looking at Masco itself and its leaders. Surely, the ultimate fault lies there. But to get the full picture, you must look as much outside as inside the firm.

Here is a first clue.

As our faculty team was preparing to teach the case for the first time, a colleague, the most senior in the room, said, "Wait a minute. This story sounds very familiar." He left the meeting and went back to his office files. There he found "Mengel Company (A)," a case so old it was typed on onionskin paper.

Set in 1946, the Mengel case describes the firm's plans to revolutionize the highly fragmented furniture industry. Mengel's bold idea? Build scale, gain efficiencies by leveraging its manufacturing skills, and establish brand identity. To do this, it would buck industry practice and spend $500,000 on national advertising to "make the average consumer style-conscious" and build its "Permanized" brand name.[3] I had never heard of Mengel, but with an eerie sense of déjà vu, I wondered if Masco's leaders had known about them.

My own research in the industry led to the following list. What do you think these seemingly disparate companies have in common?

> Consolidated Foods
> Champion International
> Mead
> General Housewares
> Ludlow
> Intermark
> Georgia Pacific
> Beatrice Foods
> Scott Paper
> Burlington Industries
> Gulf + Western

Like Mengel and Masco, these are all companies that tried and failed to find fortune in furniture manufacturing.

Most were regarded as well-run companies. Like Masco, they considered a fragmented, chaotic industry to be an opportunity for good managers to apply their skills. With great expectations and high hopes of success, they all jumped in with the intention of reshaping the industry through the infusion of "professional management." Years later, they all left.

UNDERSTANDING THE FORCES

Most executives find this list both revealing and disconcerting. These were companies with considerable track records, yet they all failed in the same endeavor. Was there something problematic about the endeavor itself? Was something at work in the furniture industry that was outside the control of these companies and their leaders?

Here's another clue.

Look at the chart on Relative Industry Profitability. It shows the average return on equity for twenty industries over the twenty-year period from 1990 to 2010. The chart was compiled from Standard & Poor's and Compustat databases that include data on all companies that traded on U.S. stock exchanges.

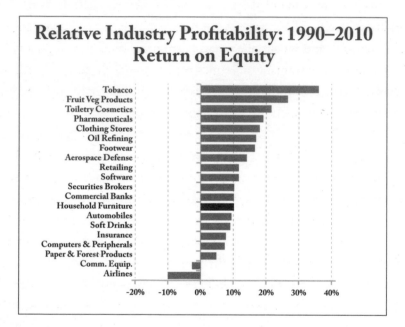

Are you surprised by how much profitability varies by industry? Compare Tobacco companies at 36.1 percent *average annual* return on equity—which means leading firms in the industry do even better—with Airlines at -10 percent or Commercial Equipment at -2 percent.

In my experience, most executives understand that average profitability will differ from industry to industry, but the scale of variation often comes as a surprise. Annual average returns in the most profitable industries are well more than double those in median industries, and more than four or five times those at the bottom of the distribution.

Researchers have found similar differences in other countries, in both advanced and emerging economies.[4]

Are these vast differences from industry to industry caused by random variation? It's not likely—they're too large and too consistent. Do some types of businesses attract great managers while others attract only poor ones? Sometimes, but not enough to account for the differences.

In fact, these variations are caused by economic forces that shape each industry's competitive landscape differently.[5] As Michael Porter has shown, some of these relate to the nature of rivalry within the industry itself; others have to do with the balance of power between the industry and its suppliers and customers, substitute products, and potential new entrants. Sometimes the forces are fierce and lead to low levels of industry profitability; other times they're relatively benign and set the scene for much more profitable outcomes.

The collective impact of these forces on the profitability of individual firms, and, in turn, on industries in which they operate, is called the industry effect. You may be surprised to learn that some and perhaps much of your company's performance is determined by such forces.[6]

These competitive forces are beyond the control of most individual companies and their managers. They're what you inherit, a reality that you have to deal with. It's not that a firm can never change them, but in most cases it's very difficult to do. The strategist's first job is to understand them and how they affect the playing field where competition takes place.

MAKING THE DISTINCTIONS

As suggested by the above chart, industries can be arrayed along a continuum extending from "Unattractive" to "Attractive," where attractiveness refers to the degree to which industry competitive forces restrict, allow, or even foster firm profitability. The table below identifies the most important of these economic forces and characterizes what they probably would be like in industries at the bounds of such a continuum.[7]

Unattractive		. . . . to Attractive
High. Many homogeneous competitors and homogeneous products. Innovations quickly copied. Slow growth. Excess capacity. Price competition.	**Rivalry among firms**	**Low.** One or a few dominant, differentiated players. Unique products. Strong brand identities. Rapid industry growth. Shortage of capacity.
High. Industry is dependent on a few, concentrated suppliers producing unique products, and Industry is not important source of profitability to suppliers.	**Power of suppliers**	**Low.** Many suppliers producing homogeneous products. Price competition and plentiful supply make it easy to procure supplies at reasonable cost.
High. Customers have lots of choice among similar products. Low levels of brand awareness. Low switching costs. Low levels of emotional involvement with purchase.	**Power of customers**	**Low.** Products are scarce, highly differentiated, and important to customers' well-being. Customers have limited choice. Brands are strong.
Low. Industry is easy to enter and sometimes difficult to exit, creating excess capacity. Strategies of existing competitors can be easily replicated or surpassed. Entry requires low levels of capital, modest scale, and no scarce or specialized resources.	**Barriers to entry and exit**	**High.** It is difficult or not economical for new firms to enter your industry. Entry requires economies of scale, product differentiation, high capital investment, regulatory approval, or accumulation of special expertise or experience.
High. Wide variety of compelling substitute products are available that meet customers' needs at attractive relative prices.	**Availability of substitute products**	**Low.** Customers have few or no choices of alternative products that could meet their needs at comparable prices.

Note how closely many of the competitive conditions in furniture manufacturing mirror those in the left-hand "Unattractive" column.

• Rivalry among furniture firms is intense, as shown by the high number of firms making similar furniture and by the ability of firms to copy innovations made by competitors.

• Suppliers to the furniture industry, such as textile makers, dominate the vendor relationship because no furniture company buys enough textiles to be an important customer.

• Customers in the industry are powerful because furniture purchases are highly postponable, products are long-lived and commodity-like, and customers are not brand sensitive.

• Entry barriers are low, meaning that new firms can flood in and pull down prices if industry conditions ever become more attractive. On the other hand, the industry can be difficult to exit, especially for the many family firms that have few alternative options, making excess capacity slow to leave the industry.

• Substitute products abound. New furniture must compete for the customer's dollar with countless alternatives—including used furniture or hand-me-down furniture passed from user to user. Since many customers consider furniture a discretionary purchase, it must also compete with a plethora of products such as televisions and sound systems that customers are more excited about and consider to be a better value for their discretionary dollars. Even when furniture prices lagged increases in the consumer price index, sales did not respond.

How do you react to the existence of these forces?

It isn't a happy lesson for many executives I teach. It seems to say, "Your prospects are predetermined—the game is up—or, if not up, a big chunk of it is out of your control." Action-oriented executives, I find, prefer not to think of themselves as in the grip of outside forces. They prefer to believe in free will, not determinism. The possibility that their industries might drive or heavily influence their own performance isn't near the top of their minds. As proactive leaders and believers in the power of management, they tend to focus on what they can control, while ignoring or underestimating what they cannot.

REJECTING THE MYTH

Ironically, the most successful and admired leaders, the titans of business, understand the profound significance of competitive forces outside their control. They know the crucial importance of picking the right playing field. They don't buy the management myth that a truly good manager can prevail regardless of the circumstances.

Look at Jack Welch, *Fortune* magazine's "Manager of the Century." You probably don't remember that when he took over General Electric, Welch sold off more than 200 businesses worth more than $11 billion and used that money to make more than 370 acquisitions. Why? He wanted out of industries where conditions were too negative, where he thought it would be too hard for GE to flourish. "I didn't like the semiconductor business," he said. "I thought it was too cyclical and it required too much capital. There were some very big players in it and only one or two were making any money on a sustained basis. . . . [Exiting that business] allowed us to put our money into things like medical equipment, power generation, all kinds of industries where we changed the game. . . ."[8]

A comment from the Sage of Omaha himself, Warren Buffett, caps the point:

> *When a management with a reputation for brilliance tackles a business with a reputation for bad economics, it is the reputation of the business that remains intact.*[9]

Buffett and Welch, two of the strongest managers on record, recognize that industry matters a lot. They understand that a significant measure of a firm's success depends on competitive forces beyond a manager's control, and they use that knowledge to their own advantage—by picking playing fields where they can win and, within those fields, carefully positioning their businesses to work with, not against, the forces.

BUT WHAT ABOUT . . . ?

Despite such counsel, the myth of the super-manager lives on for many executives. It's reinforced in practice just often enough to give it credence. Sometimes, even in the toughest lines of business, there *is* a plan that works. Individual firms on occasion have not only achieved great success in industries where most others have failed, but they've even changed the basic competitive context of the industries.

Such stories receive inordinate attention in business books and media, and executives are always quick to bring them up: Starbucks's revolution in the coffee house business. Southwest's triumphs in discount airlines. Cirque du Soleil's reinvention of the circus business. Even Masco's coup in faucets. Yes, it does happen.

But none of these strategies appeared out of the blue from the unfettered minds of super-managers. They came from a deep comprehension of the industries involved and the conditions at work in them. The founders of Southwest discovered a way to exploit a hole in the fare and route structures of established competitors. Starbucks succeeded not simply by brewing better coffee and creating an attractive coffee house experience, but by gaining scale and building the unique corporate skills needed to replicate that experience not tens or hundreds but thousands of times.

The founders of Cirque du Soleil, performers themselves, understood the essence of the traditional circus—that it was focused on children and that its economics were badly strained by the expense of transporting and caring for large, wild animals. By focusing on an *adult* audience, which let them drop many of the animal acts, they skillfully positioned themselves to avoid one of the industry's greatest drains on profits while targeting customers with the highest willingness to pay.[10] That's not a cavalier disregard for industry forces: It's surgical precision.

Look, too, at Warren Buffett's portfolio. Most people don't know he's made significant investments in furniture. Like Masco, he also saw potential in the industry. But Buffett chose to invest in furniture retailing, not manufacturing, and bought several successful furniture sellers around the United States. He seems to be experimenting to see if these downstream retailers can benefit from the intensely competitive conditions upstream in furniture manufacturing—the very conditions that brought down Masco, Mengel, and all the others. In the long run, these may not turn out to be Buffett's most brilliant ventures, but they reveal a real strategist playing his cards carefully with a deep appreciation of the forces at work in the industry.

No one can say that the decision to enter or remain in a tough industry is right or wrong on the face of it. Remaking a difficult business, as Masco set out to do, isn't easy, but as we've seen, it can and has been done. When it works, though, it's always a two-sided affair: It involves an industry, or part of an industry, that can be changed and a firm with a viable way to do so.

THE MISSING INFORMATION

What does all this tell you about Masco and its failed furniture venture?

For the full answer, we must look more closely at Masco's actions and at how most of my students—people much like you, I suspect—saw only the upside potential of the opportunity.

After a class has voted for Masco to enter furniture manufacturing (and they always do), I ask the strongest proponents of the move how the firm should proceed. What specific actions should Masco's managers take that will cause it to perform above the average in its new line of business?

Alongside the bold decision to enter, the proponents' plans usually look surprisingly lackluster. Nearly all of them start with "Masco should acquire . . ." and go on to add some grand but vague statements about rationalizing production, improving efficiency, leveraging the company's professional management, using "power marketing," and so on. When I want to know what the company would do differently, how "professional management" would work here, or what would set the firm apart from others, the answers get progressively vague and superficial. They haven't thought about all that.

What becomes clear is that their arguments are propelled by an enthusiasm for the company itself, for what it's achieved in the past, and for the storehouse of capabilities it could bring to a new venture. What is missing is a specific plan that shows why all of that will matter in this industry, and how it will neutralize the long-lived forces that have broken so many other firms.

These discussions always remind me of how French generals after World War I responded to the fact that, in the previous half century, Germany had twice defeated French armies. The generals took a number of steps, including construction of the now-infamous Maginot Line, but a key reason, they said, that France would not be defeated again was the élan vital of the French soldier. *Élan vital* means "vital spirit" and the gist of French thinking was that the superior determination or attitude of the French army would defeat whatever the Germans threw at it. Of course, we know how well that worked. It was the military equivalent of the myth of the super-manager.

Masco's vital spirit wasn't enough, either. Its leaders hoped its superior management and manufacturing skills would lead it to victory on a new front, and that the same strategy that had brought it great success in faucets would do the same in furniture. But, while similar in some ways, the two industries were different in other ways that Masco either failed to notice or appreciate.

Masco's purchases of furniture companies at three price points— low, middle, and high—reflected its belief that significant scope economies, or savings that come from producing a wide range of products, were possible in furniture. That approach had worked in faucets, where a range of products could be made in the same factory, sold through the same channels, installed by the same plumber, and often bought by the same customer for use in different locations in a house. In furniture, however, manufacturing, distribution, retailing, and customers differ dramatically from the top end of the market to the bottom, making scope economies much more difficult to achieve. Discount furniture is mass-produced and mass-marketed, while expensive furniture is largely handmade and distributed through specialty retail shops. Few customers buy furniture at both ends of the price and quality spectrum, and the products are almost never found at the same retailer.

Similarly, scale economies were difficult to come by in furniture. Even after it purchased its way to market leadership, Masco held only a paltry 7 percent of the market, compared with its 30 percent in faucets. Seven percent was unlikely to confer much, if any, economic advantage, particularly when spread across so many styles, so many manufacturing plants, so many channels, and so many price points.

Like other furniture manufacturers, Masco's fortunes were hindered by the industry's extreme product variety, high shipping costs, and cyclicality, which in combination make it extraordinarily difficult to manage a supply chain efficiently, or profitably substitute capital equipment for labor. Without a compelling way to address these issues, a manufacturer will always be at their mercy.

Above all, Masco failed to learn the biggest lesson of its success in faucets. Its one-handle and washerless products gave it unique advantages that addressed important customer needs. Everything else it did in that industry flowed from those key differences. In a market where functionality was crucial, Masco had a demonstrable product edge. In furniture, an industry ruled more by fashion than function, Masco had no such core advantage, *nothing that was strong enough to counter the gravitational pull of the industry's unattractive competitive forces.*

Like those French generals, Masco failed to access its own battle readiness. It placed unwarranted faith in its superior management élan vital *and underestimated the forces it was up against*. One executive used a different but similar metaphor to describe what the company did: "Masco walked into a lion's den and was unprepared to meet a lion."

THE STRATEGIST IN REMORSE

Richard Manoogian, CEO-strategist and son of the company's founder, took the outcome hard. At stake wasn't merely a company he ran but the legacy his father had created and passed on to him. Father and son had strung together thirty-one years of consistently superior performance and created a superb reputation on Wall Street. All of that went up in smoke. In a story titled, "The Masco Fiasco," *Financial World* observed: "The Masco Corp. was once one of America's most admired companies; not anymore." Though Manoogian promised to return the company to "its past glory," he would have to regain the trust of his shareholders, many of whom felt "stuck in a nine-year nightmare of broken promises."[11]

It was a case of the overconfident strategist. Along with many other companies that tried to crack the furniture industry, Masco believed a disorganized, competitive, low-profit business offered easy prospects for a disciplined, well-managed company. By some process of optimistic thinking, superficial analysis, and misplaced analogy, serious industry problems began to look like golden opportunities.

The same hopeful thinking reappears every time I teach the Masco case. In their initial analysis of the furniture business, my students—all seasoned executives—duly note how unattractive it is. Yet when the time comes to decide what Masco should do, they prefer to interpret every problem as an opportunity (an "insurmountable opportunity," as some wag once said). Chaos, cyclicality, fragmentation? Great! No dominant player and low brand recognition? Wonderful! A difficult-to-manage supply chain with large, expensive items, and huge variety? Terrific! Seemingly, there was nothing Masco's resources and prowess could not overcome or turn to their advantage. It is the myth of the super-manager in full force.

I suspect Masco fell into the same trap. In the face of deeply ingrained, long-lived industry problems, its leaders succumbed to a costly bout of irrational faith in the power of superior management.

THE POWER OF REALISM

Do the lessons of Masco resonate with you?

More than twenty years after the Masco fiasco, my students repeatedly approach me to say, "My industry is just like the furniture business! I'm working really hard and getting nowhere." For them it's a eureka moment. The issues they've been battling suddenly come into focus, and they understand the larger reasons for their struggles.

They, like Welch, Buffett, and other astute business leaders, grasp the lesson of the industry effect and its profound implications for firm performance. They recognize that, as in the famous serenity prayer, you must accept the things you cannot change, have the courage to change the things you can, and the wisdom to know the difference. It's a lesson great strategists understand well, but it's not an easy lesson to accept and master. The myth of the super-manager is hard to let go.

The fundamental lessons here are simple but of paramount importance for the strategist.

First, you must understand the competitive forces in your industry. How you respond to them is your strategy. That means if you don't understand them, your strategy is based on luck and hope.

Second, even if you understand your industry's competitive forces, you must find a way to deal with them that is up to the challenge. That may mean skillful positioning, deliberate efforts to counter negative forces or exploit favorable ones, or even a timely exit. But don't be trapped by the myth into believing that your superior management skills will carry you to success.

Third, whatever you do, don't underestimate the power of these forces. Their impact on the destiny of your business may well be as great as your own.

The story you will write as a strategist will be set against the backdrop of your industry. It must be true to its realities, while having a difference that's all its own. It's to the second of these challenges that we now turn.

4

BEGIN WITH PURPOSE

WE'VE LEARNED SOME painful lessons about the challenges that confront strategists in the face of unattractive industry forces. With this chapter, I begin mapping the path out of the wilderness: specifically, explaining how some astute strategists have managed to distinguish their businesses even in the face of such headwinds.

The journey starts with an individual: Ingvar Kamprad, the founder of IKEA who by all accounts built one of the world's greatest fortunes. Like Richard Manoogian of Masco, Kamprad was in the furniture business, but his story couldn't be more different. In 2010, his privately held company, which he started in 1943 at the age of seventeen, had sales of 23.1 billion euro, net profits of 2.5 billion euro, and gross margins of 46 percent.

And the numbers don't even begin to capture IKEA's powerful hold on consumers. As *BusinessWeek* put it, "Perhaps more than any other company in the world, IKEA has become a curator of people's lifestyles, if not their lives. IKEA World [is] a state of mind that revolves around contemporary design, low prices, wacky promotions, and an enthusiasm that few institutions in or out of business can muster."[1]

How did Kamprad succeed where Manoogian failed? He built his company by creating what I like to call a *difference that matters*. (The full meaning of this phrase will become clear as the story unfolds.) He did so, not by ignoring industry forces, as Manoogian did, but by creating a company that could thrive and add value in the midst of them.

If you're one of the millions who have shopped at IKEA, you'll likely have indelible memories of vast, bright, modern stores designed so that entering customers follow a winding path through a huge building filled with furnishings and a great miscellany of housewares. When you chose a piece of furniture—a simple Micke desk for 69 euro, or a ten-person Norden dining table for 269 euro—you noted the information on an order slip, continued on the path to a warehouse-like room, wrestled a flat box containing the item onto your shopping trolley, carted it home on the rooftop of your car, and assembled it yourself. If you brought the kids, you may have parked them in the on-site child care center; you may also have stopped at the restaurant to sample tasty and inexpensive food ranging from salmon to Swedish meatballs and lingonberry tarts. It's almost a theme park: probably not a customer experience you'd relish if you've made your fortune, but when you were starting out, there was nothing that could match it.

RURAL ROOTS

One could say that Ingvar Kamprad was a natural-born entrepreneur. "Trading was in my blood" he told his biographer, Bertil Torekull.[2] Kamprad was about five when his aunt helped him buy a hundred boxes of matches from a store in Stockholm that he then sold individually at a profit in his rural hometown of Agunnaryd, deep in the farmland of Smaland. Soon he was selling all sorts of merchandise: Christmas cards, wall hangings, lingonberries (he picked them himself), fish (which he caught), and more. At eleven, he made enough money to buy a bicycle and typewriter. "From that time on," he recounted, "selling things became something of an obsession."[3]

Before going to the School of Commerce in Gothenburg, Kamprad signed the paperwork to start his own trading firm, IKEA Agunnaryd [I for Ingvar, K for Kamprad, E for the family farm Elmtaryd, and A for Agunnaryd]. The mail-order business grew to include everything from fountain pens and picture frames to watches and jewelry. With a keen eye for value, Kamprad ferreted out the lowest-cost sources. Frugality was the norm in Smaland. Its farmers, eking their living from a harsh and spare environment, had to make every penny count.

Noticing that his toughest competitor in the catalog business sold furniture, Kamprad decided to add some to his offerings, supplied by small local furniture makers. Furniture quickly became the biggest part of his business; in the postwar boom, Swedes were buying a lot of it. In 1951, at age twenty-five, he dropped all his other products to focus exclusively on furniture.

Almost immediately he found himself in a crisis. Growing competition from other mail-order firms led to a price war. Across the industry, quality dropped as merchants and manufacturers cut costs. Complaints started to mount. "The mail order trade was risking an increasingly bad reputation," Kamprad said.[4] He didn't want to join the race to the bottom, but how could he persuade customers that his goods were sound when they had only catalog descriptions to rely on? His answer: create a showroom where customers could see the merchandise firsthand. In 1953 he opened one in an old two-story building. The furniture was on the ground floor; upstairs were free coffee and buns. Over a thousand people came to the village for the opening, and a gratifying number wrote out orders. By 1955, IKEA was sending out a half a million catalogs and had sales of 6 million krona.

Kamprad understood his customers on a personal level. As he would later say, in explaining IKEA's philosophy, "Since IKEA turns to the many people who as a rule have small resources, the company must be not just cheap, nor just cheaper—but very much cheaper . . . the goods must be such that ordinary people can easily and quickly identify the lowness of the price."[5]

By following this philosophy, Kamprad became a force to contend with in the Swedish furniture industry—and, not liking his low prices, the industry struck back. Sweden's National Association of Furniture Dealers began pressuring suppliers to boycott him and, with the support of the Stockholm Chamber of Commerce, banned him from trade fairs. Many of the suppliers stopped selling to him, and those that continued to do business with IKEA resorted to cloak-and-dagger maneuvers: sending goods to fictitious addresses, delivering in unmarked vans, and changing the design of products sold to IKEA so they wouldn't be recognized. Soon Kamprad was suffering the humiliation of not being able to deliver on orders.

He counterattacked on several fronts—for example, he began paying suppliers within ten days, as opposed to the standard industry practice of three or four months, and he started a flock of little companies to act as intermediaries. These moves helped, but IKEA was growing rapidly and supplies were short. Without a reliable source of supply, Kamprad feared his business would be doomed.

Having heard that Poland's communist government was hungry for economic development, Kamprad began scouring the Polish countryside. He found many eager and willing small manufacturers laboring in the shadow of the bureaucracy. Their plants were antiquated and the quality of their products was dreadful, so Kamprad located better-quality (though used) machinery in Sweden. He and his staff moved the machinery to Poland and installed it, working hand in hand with the manufacturers to raise productivity and quality. The furniture they turned out ended up costing about half as much as Swedish-made equivalents and Kamprad was able to nail down his costs on a huge new scale.

Thus the boycott turned out to be what I call an "inciting incident," to borrow a phrase from screenwriter Robert McKee—an event that propelled a critical strategic shift.[6] "New problems created a dizzying chance," Kamprad said. "When we were not allowed to buy the same furniture others were, we were forced to design our own, and that came to provide us with a style of our own, a design of our own. And from the necessity to secure our own deliveries, a chance arose that in its turn opened up a whole new world to us."[7]

To Kamprad, it wasn't enough to simply source in developing countries. He also brought extraordinary determination and imagination to his drive for lower costs. For example, he wasn't afraid to draw on unconventional sources. He turned the job of making a particular table over to a ski manufacturer, who could deliver it at an especially low price. He bought headboards from a door factory, and wire-framed sofas and tables from a maker of shopping carts. IKEA was also a pioneer in building "board-on-frame furniture," comprised of finished wood on a particleboard core, which is both cheaper and lighter than solid wood.

Then, of course, there is the iconic IKEA packaging—the famous flat pack with its do-it-yourself assembly. While the company didn't invent this approach, it was the first to grasp and systematically exploit its full potential. The flat pack provides huge cost savings by making shipping, distribution, and storage much more efficient and thus much cheaper. It saves manufacturing steps; it saves shipping costs from factory to store; it saves stocking and handling costs in the store; and it eliminates delivery costs for most customers.

IKEA opened its first store in 1958 in Almhult. Five years later it opened one in Norway, and two years after that, a second Swedish store in Stockholm. It became a nascent global player with openings in Switzerland in 1973 and Germany in 1974. It entered the United States in 1985, China in 1998, Russia in 2000, and Japan in 2006. In 2010, IKEA had 280 stores in twenty-six countries, and served 626 million visitors.[8]

BEYOND LOW PRICES

So how do you account for IKEA's success in this terrible industry? Most likely your immediate thought is "low prices, low prices, low prices." Indeed, IKEA's prices are so low they're not just a difference in degree from competitors' but a difference in kind.

Over the past decade, the company has lowered its prices by 2 to 3 percent a year on average. Every aspect of IKEA's operation is subject to ongoing scrutiny to see where further costs can be taken out. Even flat packs have been repeatedly redesigned to gain small efficiencies in the use of space. Kamprad regarded the customary perks of business leadership as waste, too. Stories are legend of his flying coach class or taking a bus instead of a taxi or limousine. It's an attitude that's been adopted wholeheartedly by others in the company who speak of spending money unnecessarily as a "disease, a virus that eats away at otherwise healthy companies."[9]

But IKEA is not a dollar store: Low prices don't begin to tell the whole story. Scandinavian design was becoming popular around the world in the 1950s and it suited IKEA's strategy perfectly. The simplicity of the clean lines made the furnishings particularly appealing; it also made them cheaper to produce than more ornate designs. Kamprad pushed this envelope farther, hiring first-class talent who could design for both style and for frugal manufacturing techniques. Perhaps IKEA's greatest design achievement has been to make its furniture look and feel more expensive than it is. A turning point came in 1964 when a respected Swedish furniture magazine compared IKEA furniture with more highly regarded brands. IKEA's, it found, was often as good or better. That shocked the industry and helped to persuade consumers that they had nothing to lose—either financially or in terms of status—by shopping at IKEA.

Unlike so many discount retail stores, IKEA's are anything but dark and dingy. The company's vibrant colors (mostly blue and yellow, the colors of the Swedish flag) are everywhere, and except for the weekend crowds, the stores are pleasant places to visit. You can make a day of it: Come with the family, try out the sofas, use the computerized tools to design your own kitchen, and have a full-fledged Swedish meal at the restaurant. If, at the end of the day, you've bought too much to load onto your car, you can rent an IKEA van to drive it all home, or even pay to have things delivered, assembled, and set up.

So, what is it that is special about IKEA? I ask you. Low price? Design? Flat pack? Swedish meatballs? What? The answer, of course, is "all of the above." The centerpiece is low cost—without that, nothing else works—but everything else not only supports low cost but adds its own distinctive attraction.

At this point, you, like many managers, may feel like, "Okay, we're done—we've cracked the case. We know the answer, time to move on." Maybe so. But what is the real lesson here? What do you take with you to apply to your company? That low cost with some added distinctive features is a winning combination?

Often it is.

But what if I tell you there is a deeper insight here, an insight that applies to all businesses whether you've decided to compete on low price or with differentiated, specialty products. It's something else that was behind *everything* IKEA did.

A CONCEPT COMPANY

If Ingvard Kamprad were here and we asked him to describe the essence of what IKEA was doing, what would he say?

His own words are instructive: "We are a concept company." He goes on to describe the idea that guides the firm. IKEA offers *"a wide range of well-designed, functional home furnishing products at prices so low that as many people as possible will be able to afford them."* This serves the company's aim to create *"a better everyday life for the many."*[10]

These words weren't said by Kamprad on rare occasions. He said them often, over and over. He wrote them out, and more like them, in statements and booklets he printed and distributed to employees. All new employees are indoctrinated with these ideas, and they're prominent in the company's annual report today.

Although IKEA calls this statement its "concept," the word I prefer is *purpose. Purpose* is the way IKEA or any other company describes itself in the most fundamental terms possible—why it exists, the unique value it brings to the world, what sets it apart, and why and to whom it matters. Notice how IKEA's purpose as expressed above answers all these questions.

I suspect, though, that some of you, like some EOPers, are leery of lofty prose. Perhaps you consider Kamprad's words mostly PR fluff—fancy words to dress up a hard-nosed, cost-cutting approach. But these words don't just "dress up" low prices. On the contrary, they are what drive IKEA's low prices and all the other features that make it stand out.

To underline the point, consider something else Kamprad wrote in "A Furniture Dealer's Testament," a document he prepared to keep the growing company focused on what it was all about:

> *We have decided once and for all to side with the many. . . . The many usually have limited financial resources. It is the many whom we aim to serve. The first rule is to maintain an extremely low level of prices. But they must be low prices with a meaning. We must not compromise either functionality or technical quality.*[11]

So it wasn't low prices alone that drove IKEA. Low prices weren't the goal but rather a means to an end: "low prices with a meaning"—a better everyday life for the many.

What was Masco's purpose in furniture? It didn't really have one, did it—other than a vague belief that it would have some sort of scale advantage and would bring professional management skills and capabilities to an industry that sorely lacked them. In contrast, IKEA's clear and compelling purpose addressed a long-lived market need, created a distinctive niche, and mattered a lot to its customers.

As you mull the idea of corporate purpose, you may make the connection to the more familiar "competitive advantage." In fact, the terms *purpose* and *competitive advantage* could be used in conjunction with each other, but competitive advantage places the focus on a firm's competition. That's important, but it's not enough. Leaders too often think the heart of strategy is beating the competition. Not so. Strategy is about serving an unmet need, doing something unique or uniquely well for some set of stakeholders. Beating the competition is critical, to be sure, but it's the result of finding and filling that need, not the goal.

Consider the power of purpose and the differences it spawns across firms. In the last chapter we looked at the average profitability of different industries as a whole. We treated each industry as if it were a single entity, and showed the *average* profitability of firms in each industry, the *industry effect*. Here we consider the variation in profitability *within* an industry, across players. This is the *firm effect*—the difference between an individual firm's profitability and the average profitability in its industry. Positive or negative, large or small, it's the sum of the impact of all a firm's actions.

Firm effects are directly tied to the work of a strategist, and over the long run are one of the best indicators of success or failure on the job. Within an industry, they can vary widely, even though most of the players work in a similar context and face largely the same competitive forces (See Exhibit 4-1, below). In tobacco, for example, Imperial Tobacco and Altria have returns that are even higher than the industry average, giving them positive firm effects. Reynolds American and others, in contrast, have negative firm effects. In airlines, Ryanair and Southwest buck the negative industry return while many of their competitors fare far, far worse.

How Firms Differ: Firm Effects in Four Industries

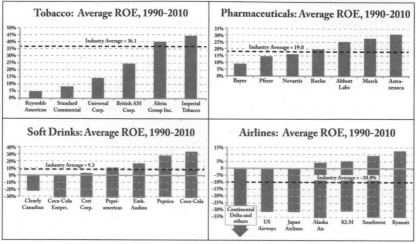

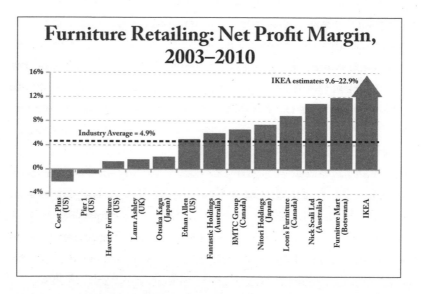

The chart on Furniture Retailing shows the net profit margin for a number of furniture retailers around the globe. Average profits in the industry are low (4.9 percent), but some firms do better than the average, and IKEA (whole returns are estimates) is at or near the top of the pack.[12]

The key question: What explains the firm effect that creates such differences among players in an industry? What can lead a company like IKEA to excel even in a business as tough as this?

The answer, I believe, begins with purpose. Purpose is where performance differences start. Nothing else is more important to the survival and success of a firm than why it exists, and what otherwise unmet needs it intends to fill. It is the first and most important question a strategist must answer. Every concept of strategy that has entered the conversation of business managers—sustainable competitive advantage, positioning, differentiation, added value, even the firm effect—flows from purpose.

EFFECTIVE PURPOSES

All this sounds attractive to the leaders I've worked with. It seems to lift their work above the dog-eat-dog world of cutthroat competition and harsh reality. Most of them want to feel that what they do matters in some context larger than themselves and larger even than their companies. They want to play their roles on as large a stage as possible. And so they embrace the idea of purpose because it feels inspiring. And, as we'll see, that's part of it. But to be a serious guide for a company, a purpose needs to do much more.

A good purpose is ennobling. It makes a firm's endeavors noble or more dignified. In addition to its other merits, a good purpose can satisfy this need. It is inspiring to all involved, to the employees pursuing it, to customers, and to others in your value chain. The people at IKEA don't believe they're flogging cheap furniture. They believe they're creating "a better everyday life" for the many people who can't afford top-end furnishings.

In a Gallup poll nearly all respondents said it is "very important" or "fairly important" to them to "believe life is meaningful or has a purpose," but less than half of the workers in any industry felt strongly connected to their organization's purpose. Equally interesting, a number of people in less than life-and-death careers (for example, septic tank pumping, retail trades, chemical manufacturing) felt a strong connection to the goals of their organizations, while others in some traditional "helping" fields (for example, hospital workers) felt far less connection. An analysis of the work concluded:

> *There is no such thing as an inherently meaningless job. There are conditions that make the seemingly most important roles trivial and conditions that make ostensibly awful work rewarding. . . . The least engaged group sees their work as simply a job: a necessary inconvenience and a way of earning money with which they can accomplish personal goals and enjoy themselves outside of work.*[13]

Don't overlook the role of purpose in fostering the care and commitment that lead people to produce good results. Consider a business forms company that sells its services to small businesses. You can't get much more mundane than invoices and sales slips, but the people there said: "What we do isn't glamorous, but it's essential. When you can't pay people or give the customer a receipt, the business stops running."

A good purpose puts a stake in the ground. It says "We do X, not Y." "We will be this, not that." It's a commitment.

Choosing to be one thing means not being something else. Michael Porter recognized that such choices involve trade-offs—letting some things go in order to be better at something else.[14] Companies that don't choose, for whatever reason, run the risk of ending up in no-man's-land, being nothing of distinction to anyone. If your purpose does not preclude you from undertaking certain kinds of work, then it's not a good purpose. Purpose, like strategy, is about choice, and a real choice contains, if only implicitly, both positive ("We do this") and negative ("By implication, then, we don't do something else") elements.

One executive I worked with in the EOP program, Pedro Guimaraes, a CEO of a small but growing movie production company, discovered this only after he clarified his purpose. His firm was primarily backed by an angel investor, a woman who had become very wealthy from her own business ventures and now, through this company, was pursuing a longtime personal love of movies and culture in general. As part of our work in the program, Pedro wrote out his purpose for the company, describing how it would make money through the production of advertising and movies that were commercial successes.

When he showed the purpose to his investor, he discovered what had only been simmering under the surface of their relationship. He wanted to produce top-grossing box-office hits and make profits. She had little interest in those and instead, primarily wanted to produce art films, the kind once made by Ingmar Bergman in Sweden or Federico Fellini in Italy. At that moment he finally understood why the investor had balked at a number of projects he had proposed. From the outset they had been on different pages, but had never dug deeply enough into their respective purposes to see the incompatibility. They parted company amicably, and each went on to ventures that were more consistent with their different aims.

A good purpose sets you apart; it makes you distinct. If you can only describe your business generically—"We're a PR firm" or "We're an IT consulting company"—then you don't have a real purpose. Somehow the reason you exist, the specific customers you've chosen to serve, the market needs you fill, must set you apart from others who generically do what you do. Generically, IKEA is a furniture retailer, but that description doesn't begin to say why it matters or what distinguishes it from others in the industry. Here is how IKEA describes its difference:

> *From the beginning, IKEA has taken a different path. . . . It's not difficult to manufacture expensive fine furniture. Just spend the money and let the customers pay. To manufacture beautiful, durable furniture at low prices is not so easy. It requires a different*

approach. Finding simple solutions, scrimping and saving in every
direction. Except on ideas.[15]

Where do differences come from? They arise from innovation, new
ideas, and deep insights about how things are and how they could be
better in some consequential way. These can be anything from a new
production technology that enhances efficiency, to new, different, and
more appealing products, to a change in the way products or services are
sold or delivered. Sometimes what matters is not just one innovation,
but a cluster of innovations that flow from a new concept, a new way
of doing business. This was the case for IKEA. Its greatest innovations
were not in original furniture designs, or even in the technical invention
of the flat pack, but in a new idea of how to go to market and how to
provide a set of customers with products and a shopping experience that
met their needs resoundingly well.

IKEA's experience illustrates a key advantage of a good purpose. A
clear sense of what a company is striving to do can serve as a focal point
or a core organizing principle around which a whole set of innovations
and distinctive features can coalesce.

Above all, a good purpose sets the stage for value creation and
capture.

Good economics are not the only reason your business exists, but
without them, it's unlikely that any of your other goals will be realized.

Whatever your purpose, it must mean something to others in
ways that produce good economic outcomes for you. What made
IKEA's purpose so powerful was not just that it was distinctive or
well-defined, or that it made people feel part of something bigger
and more important. It also drove IKEA's superior performance in
its industry.

ADDING VALUE FOR EVERYONE

The acid test, then, of a purpose is this: Will it give you a difference that *matters* in your industry?

Not all differences are equal. You need a difference with real consequences. I often see companies claim differences that in fact are simply points of distinction without much consequence in their industries—"one-stop shopping," "oldest continually operated," "largest independent supplier." Even a legitimate difference such as "best-in-class quality" is often rendered meaningless by companies that trumpet the words but don't make the investments or tough trade-offs such a goal requires.

IKEA's purpose set it up to deal with the industry forces that scuttled Masco and many others in the furniture business. The company took two of the industry's biggest problems—price competition and customers' low willingness to pay—and made them a virtue through specific techniques such as lean manufacturing, the flat pack, and store design. It dealt with the industry's costly practice of manufacturing a huge variety of furnishings by selling a limited selection of furniture pieces within one style.

Many people think about strategy as a zero-sum game between a firm and its competitors, suppliers, and customers: How do we win? How do we get what's best for us? In doing so, they largely focus on the sphere that's closest to home: increasing their own profits—through higher prices or lower costs. On the Added Value chart, it's the region called "Value captured by firm."[16]

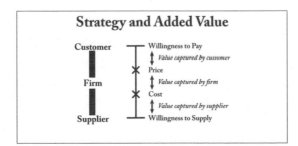

Strategy and Added Value

A trio of economists[17]—Adam Brandenburger, Barry Nalebuff, and Harborne Stuart—who study game theory suggest a wider angle. They remind us that managers need to think not only about what's best for their own firms, but also about how what they do affects others. This involves the two outer lines: Customers' Willingness to Pay (essentially customers' satisfaction with a good or service) and Suppliers' Willingness to Supply (essentially their opportunity cost—the lowest price at which they would be willing to sell to a particular firm). It's when a company drives a wider wedge between these lines—expanding the total value created—that its existence matters in an industry. When it does so, it is much more likely to be able to claim some of the value for itself—i.e., increase its own profitability—without making its partners in trade less well off.

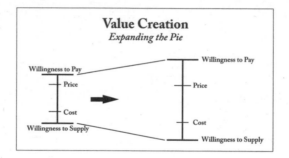

Value Creation
Expanding the Pie

Wal-Mart is a classic example. It offers its customers good quality products at considerably lower prices, increasing the value customers capture from the relationship. At the same time, Wal-Mart lowers its own costs by lowering the costs of its suppliers. It does this by buying in scale, sharing information, and taking costs out of *their* systems.

There are interesting parallels between Sam Walton and Ingvar Kamprad—for example, they both nurtured their vision of low-cost retailing in backwaters, where they learned how to court customers without much money. The most important parallel, though, from the standpoint of strategy, is that they both understood the benefits of adding value through one's existence, not just fighting over who gets the biggest share of the pie.

As it was growing into the company it has become, IKEA helped its suppliers save money. It designed furniture to be less expensive to manufacture. Its flat-pack approach eliminated significant shipping and assembly costs. It ordered in volume and provided data that made its suppliers more efficient. For suppliers, all of these drove down the costs of doing business with IKEA, and, in turn, reduced the price at which they were willing to sell to the firm.

There's still more to IKEA's difference that matters. Through design and the distinctiveness of its approach, it created name recognition in a business not known for strong brands. It broke an ancient tradition of furniture as a long-term investment, and promoted the view of furniture as fashion. And it countered customers' general reluctance to shop for furniture by providing free child care and low-priced restaurants with good food, both of which increased the length of time people spent in the store.[18] So IKEA created value all around: Vendors could produce and sell for less, customers were pleased with the experience yet able to pay less, and IKEA was able to capture some of that value itself.

Successful premium-priced players, like BMW or Disney, create value differently. Their goal is to provide uncommonly good products or services that command high prices and generate particularly high levels of customer satisfaction. To do so, they typically incur higher-than-average costs that are more than compensated for by increases in customers' willingness to pay.

For any firm, however, the logic is the same: You create value by driving the widest wedge you can between the satisfaction of your customers and the all-in costs of your suppliers.[19] That means not only moving your own costs or prices relative to others in the industry, but moving one or both of those outer lines as well.

Viable purposes, worthy of guiding everything else that happens in a company, must matter not only to you but also to those with whom you do business. Creating value for others is the surest way to capture some yourself.

DOES *YOUR* BUSINESS MATTER?

It's not as easy as you might think to know whether your business has a viable purpose, or whether it truly adds value in your industry. Financial success at any given moment is an indication, but may prove fleeting. However, there is one simple question[20] that—if you can answer it honestly—will give you a good idea. In essence, it's the one I asked you at the start of this book:

If your company disappeared today, would the world be different tomorrow? Despite our long discussions about purpose, and their general buy-in to the idea, this question always catches EOP executives by surprise. Frankly, it's not a question most have been asked or asked themselves. It's a real soul-searcher. But it's one I hope you recognize that you need to answer.

Here's what it means to be different in a way that matters in your industry. It means that, if you disappear, there will be a hole in the world, a tear in the universe of those you serve, your customers. It means customers or suppliers won't be able to go out and immediately find someone else to take your place.

If you don't have that difference, nobody will mourn you when you're gone.

And if they won't miss you then, how *much* do they need you now?

One more question: Whose job is it to find an answer, to make sure there's an answer?

It's your job, the job of the strategist, the leader who's responsible for the success and survival of the firm.

It may not be the job of the strategist to invent a firm's purpose on the lonely mountaintop and then come down and deliver it. Many people may be involved in its creation. But whether there is a purpose and whether that purpose is viable is a leader's first responsibility.

This is the strategist's job.

Are you a strategist?

5

TURN PURPOSE INTO REALITY

AS THE IKEA story demonstrates, defining a sound and distinctive purpose for your business is essential. It is a strategist's way to stake a claim. With it, you have earned the right to play, to take part in the game.

But winning the game? That takes more.

Consider the experience of Domenico De Sole, an Italian-born, Harvard-trained tax attorney who in 1994-95 was thrust into the top job at Gucci.[1] Though he had previously led the company's North American operations, he was stunned by what he discovered when he saw the entirety of the once-admired company. Sales were plummeting, customers were indifferent, and red ink was flowing. Internally, Gucci had reached a state of paralysis: Management was balkanized and people were scared to make important decisions, even about such basic issues as guaranteeing a supply of bamboo handles for Gucci's signature handbag. "There was no merchandise, no pricing, no word processors, no bamboo handles. It was crazy!" he said later. Though there were impressive handbag designs, "the company couldn't produce them or deliver them."[2]

Gucci, once a symbol of high fashion and inspired design, had lost its way so badly that the investors who owned it wanted out. An effort to sell the company had failed after the bids were deemed too paltry to accept, so the investment group asked De Sole to put the house in order and sell the company's shares to the public—as soon as possible.

De Sole somehow had to create value in a failing company that was operating in a notoriously difficult industry. Clearly a strong purpose alone, no matter how well crafted, was not going to solve his many pressing problems. He needed a broader range of tools to stop the bleeding and restore Gucci's luster.

When I introduce De Sole and the Gucci challenge to the EOP executives, some of them are always dismayed. Eyebrows raise. They look to one another and to me, as if to ask: "Gucci? The designer fashion industry? Are you sure that's relevant to us?" I understand their concerns. For one thing, many of these managers view the world of fashion as almost an outlier, so much about glamor and celebrity that it is not subject to the laws of real markets. But in a high-profile, high-margin industry that has grown over the decades despite its sensitivity to economic downturns, Gucci's revival is a story of triumph and outstanding management. It didn't *just* come back, it soared back in what is widely regarded as a spectacular business turnaround.

The lessons it offers for strategists are timeless. Sooner or later, nearly all leaders will wrestle with at least some of De Sole's challenges. And the tools he used to navigate his way toward winning were just as valuable and meaningful when Gucci was once again clicking on all cylinders as they were when the business was foundering.

A BELLMAN'S LEGACY

To understand the crossroads where De Sole stood, it helps to understand the company's history.

Guccio Gucci opened his first leather goods workshop-cum-store in Florence, Italy, in 1923, focusing on fine artisanship and a standard of quality shaped by his years working as a bellman in London's Savoy Hotel, where he absorbed the impeccable taste of the very rich and very famous. The formula proved successful, and as his business grew, he built a reputation for products of style and beauty. At the urging of his son Aldo, Gucci expanded the business to Rome, Milan, and, in 1953, to New York. Just two weeks later, Guccio Gucci died.

With Aldo at the helm, brother Rodolfo in charge of the successful Milan operation, and brother Vasco running the factory in Florence, the company's growth was nothing short of phenomenal. The post–World War II period saw a new appetite for luxury goods in the developed world, along with the economic growth to pay for them, and Gucci products represented classic style "handmade" for a savvy elite.

"Quality is remembered long after price is forgotten" was how Aldo put it, embossing the statement in gold letters on pigskin plaques displayed in Gucci stores. The great movie star beauties of the day, like Sophia Loren and Grace Kelly, were photographed carrying Gucci bags. Eleanor Roosevelt and the queen of England were known to favor Gucci umbrellas. The label conferred the status of belonging in the same company as these women and showed that you had the means to buy something exquisite. Women from Beverly Hills to London, from Paris to Tokyo packed the stores, an enthusiasm that lasted through much of the 1970s.

So, I ask my students and you, where was Gucci fitting into its competitive landscape? How was it drawing in customers and keeping profits up?

For the answer, it's instructive to look at what can be thought of as a *profit frontier*,[3] a visual map that weighs a customer's willingness to pay a high or low price for particular products against a company's ability to produce those products at a high or low cost. For instance, a company that sells products at the lowest prices in an industry must, by necessity, keep its costs extremely low, or it's off the frontier. A company like Gucci can afford higher costs only if its customers are willing to pay generous prices. According to Michael Porter, the frontier can be

thought of "as the maximum value that a company delivering a particular product or service can create at a given cost, using the best available
technologies, skills, management techniques, and purchased inputs."[4]

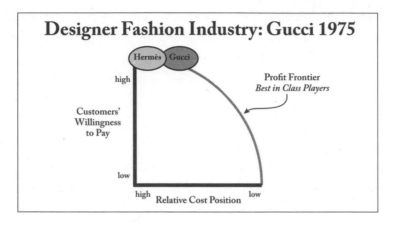

Companies actually *on* the profit frontier represent best in class; for
every price, they are the most efficient producers. Those off the frontier
are less efficient and less able to differentiate their products or services.
They are at sea in an industry defined and dominated by companies on
the frontier.

   Through the 1970s, Gucci was on the upper left-hand corner of
the frontier; it stood with Hermès and Chanel in a high-cost, high-
willingness-to-pay position, its brand resonating with elegance, wealth,
and success. But the company began unraveling after the death of Vasco
Gucci in 1975. Aldo and Rodolfo then each held 50 percent of the company. Aldo, however, believed that he had put far more into building the
family business than his brother had and resented that the two shared
ownership equally. He wanted more, and to get it, he developed another
company under the Gucci umbrella.

   The new business, 80 percent of which was owned by Aldo and his
three sons, produced a line of small canvas items sporting the Gucci
logo and trimmed in leather with striped webbing. The Gucci Accesso-

ries Collection, as the business was called, would reach a wider range of consumers, develop and license new product lines distributed through a new set of channels, and extend the reach of the Gucci brand. Launched in 1979 and managed by Aldo's son, Roberto, the accessories collection turned out to be a surprisingly lucrative venture, realizing abundant revenue for virtually no expense, primarily via licensing arrangements.

TOO MANY COOKS

This seemingly simple solution would turn into a fiasco—and soon a vendetta worthy of a *Sopranos* episode. "All happy families are alike," wrote Tolstoy; "every unhappy family is unhappy in its own way." He could have added a whole other category of family dynamics—that of a family-owned company, a situation that often challenges both companies and families.

The new accessories collection spurred another of Aldo's sons, Paolo, to develop his own line of cheaper products for younger customers, an initiative his father took extreme measures to stop. In retaliation, Paolo contacted the U.S. Internal Revenue Service, informing it that his father, then on the brink of becoming a U.S. citizen, had been cheating on his taxes, which helped send the eighty-one-year-old man to prison. Paolo also tried to tar his cousin Maurizio, Rodolfo's son, with the same charge, and Maurizio fled to Switzerland. The Italian newspaper *La Repubblica* wrote: "G isn't for Gucci, but for *Guerra*," the word for war in Italian.[5]

With the Gucci family now in turmoil and very often in court, items with the Gucci name proliferated like some kind of illness-inducing bacteria. Unbridled licensing plastered the name, along with the red-and-green logo, on sneakers, packs of playing cards, whiskey—in fact, on a total of 22,000 different products. As *Women's Wear Daily* later declared, it had become a "cheapened and overexposed brand."[6] Worse, Gucci's less expensive items were far easier to counterfeit than its fine leather goods. You could buy Gucci knockoffs anywhere—from the back alleys of Bangkok to discount stores in Denver. Now everyone could have a Gucci bag or travel with Gucci luggage, so long as you didn't mind carrying fakes—and millions of people did not. The family sued to stop production of counterfeit Gucci toilet paper but didn't bother to go to court when an enterprising shopping bag manufacturer created a Goochy line of products.

Each family member wanted a piece of the action and pursued it in his own way. In Aldo's view, however, it seemed logical to keep everything in the family—in fact, he boasted about it: "We are like an Italian trattoria," he said; "the whole family is in the kitchen."[7] The simile was all too accurate; as a trattoria, Gucci was no longer at the apex of fashion's *alto cucina*, with a scarce brand that commanded a high price. Without disciplined oversight, the licensing that seemed such a good idea at the outset—a high-margin, low-cost business—undermined the company's long-standing purpose, and Gucci slid off the profit frontier and joined the morass of underperforming firms in the market.

How could it ever find its way back? What steps would you take—what strategy—to resurrect the company and rebuild Gucci's good name?

STRUGGLING TO RESTORE THE GLAMOR

Aldo was still at war with his sons when his brother Rodolfo died in 1983. Rodolfo's son, Maurizio, back from a yearlong exile in Switzerland and now clear of legal troubles, stepped to the forefront. He enlisted the financial support of Investcorp, a Bahrain-based private equity fund, and made a bid for total control of the family business. Making common cause with his cousin Paolo, Maurizio eventually was able to buy out the rest of the family.

Maurizio called a meeting of top employees in Florence to announce not just a change in leadership but a new strategic intent as well. Gucci is "like a fine racing car," he told the company's management ranks—"a Ferrari." But it had been driven for far too long like "a Cinquecento"—the tiny Fiat 500, smaller than a VW Beetle, that was the standard utility car of Italy. "As of today," Maurizio said, "Gucci has a new driver. And with the right engine, the right parts, the right mechanics, we are going to win the race!"[8]

The race the new driver intended to win was a grand prix. "Gucci has to re-conquer the image it had in its youth," Maurizio told luxury retail genius Dawn Mello as he wooed her to Italy as his creative director. "I want to bring back the glamour . . . to re-create the excitement."[9] Mello followed where Maurizio led—back in time to the heyday of Gucci's success. "Style, not fashion" was the Mello mantra for her new design team, as it sought to create items "you don't discard after a season."[10] Instead the company would consciously re-create its own classics—the products that had originally won it fame and favor. "Once it was a privilege to own a Gucci bag," said Maurizio, "and it can be again."[11]

He took drastic actions to achieve his aim, trying to cut away the years of bad decisions and poor performance. He ruthlessly reduced the 22,000 products bearing the Gucci "name" to 7,000, slashed the number of handbag styles from 350 to a more manageable 100, closed more than 800 of the thousand stores, and in January 1990, summarily shut down the Gucci Accessories Collection. He also jettisoned the wholesale and duty-free businesses, with no backup or replacement to fill the sudden emptiness.

The drastic actions had a drastic result: From 1991 to 1993 Gucci amassed losses of approximately $102 million.[12] During this period Maurizio was spending extravagantly. He helped sponsor Italy's entry into the America's Cup sailing competition, designing everything about the boat—including the crew's costumes. He rented a five-story palazzo on Piazza San Fedele in Milan for the head office, and then began a massive, five-month renovation. He also bought a sixteenth-century villa that had once belonged to Enrico Caruso, and hoped to establish a training center there—at an estimated cost of $10 million for refurbishing.

When the new collection finally did hit the stores, Maurizio wept with joy. "This is what my father worked for," he said through his tears. "This is what Gucci used to be."[13]

Soon tears of another kind would be shed. Behind the scenes, there were no cost controls, no inventories, no financial plans in place—only Maurizio's charm, which was considerable, and his marketing intuition. With all the spending, cash was tight for the design team Mello was putting together, and the company could scarcely pay its bills or meet its payroll. As cash flow slowed, Maurizio increased his spending and raised product prices to levels customers were unwilling to pay.

By 1992, when the company lost $50 million on revenue of $200 million, Investcorp had lost faith in his ability to realize his vision. The following year, with Maurizio facing both personal and financial troubles, it bought out his stake.[14] For the first time in the company's history, there was no longer a Gucci running Gucci, no longer a family member behind the famous name.

A year later, unable to sell the company, Investcorp turned to Domenico De Sole.

PRAGMATISM REPLACES INTUITION

Facing a business on life support, De Sole began to assemble a team. He promoted Tom Ford, a thirty-two-year-old junior fashion designer, to replace Dawn Mello as creative director when Mello chose to return to the United States. He also named a new production chief and a new CFO, and strengthened the international management team. Crucially, he also secured a modest cash infusion from Investcorp.

These were necessary but not sufficient steps. Before De Sole could begin to move the company forward, he and his team had to create a fresh understanding of Gucci's purpose. What could the company be? Why might it matter? What would make it special, unique, and relevant in a world awash in Hermès, Chanel, Prada, and Louis Vuitton? Should Gucci continue to strive to be a luxury brand, aimed at the upper-upper end? Or should it be something else? What could they really afford to do?

This is where the strategist has to step up, where every leader confronted with disarray, turmoil, a declining business, or surging competition faces the greatest challenge. What will this revived company be?

When we reach this point in EOP, the class looks at the profit frontier, with Gucci miles away from a sweet spot. Though Maurizio had sought to return the company to a high-cost, high-willingness-to-pay position on the frontier, he succeeded in merely shifting its position in the middle of nowhere to a high-cost company with prices consumers would not pay.

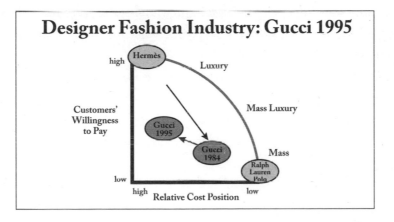

The class's instinct is to immediately jump in and take action. They're fine with Maurizio's purpose; what they want to do is a better job implementing it. I urge them to slow down and look again. "Why have we spent so much time looking at where Gucci is on this graph?" I ask them. Initially the answers are broad. "We want to see how far off course Gucci drifted," one offers. "We want to understand the past to avoid repeating the same mistakes again," offers another. After some discussion, someone finally sees the more pressing challenge. *This is where De Sole must start.* Before he can do anything to rebuild the embattled company, he must zero in on where Gucci is now, and then decide where he wants to take it. Before he can set out, he must decide where he is heading.

This is exactly what De Sole did. As Maurizio had, he summoned every Gucci manager worldwide to a meeting in Florence. But there was a crucial difference: He didn't tell them what he thought Gucci should be. Rather, he asked them to look closely at the business and tell him what was selling and what wasn't. He wanted to tackle the question "not by philosophy, but by data," by actual experience, not intuition.[15]

The data from his managers were eye-opening: Some of Gucci's greatest recent successes came from its few seasonal items. Trendier fashion, not style, was where Gucci had been getting traction. The traditional customer for whom Maurizio was so nostalgic—the woman who cherished style, not fashion, and who wanted a classic item she would buy once and keep for a lifetime—had not come back wholeheartedly to Gucci.

De Sole and Ford soberly weighed the evidence. Like Maurizio, they would have liked to keep Gucci at the top of the designer world, but they felt it was not in the cards given the reality of the situation. Regaining Gucci's elite status would take more marketing money, more design money, and more time than the company had. "We were broke," De Sole said later. "We had to be realistic about what we could do."[16]

In the end, they chose a purpose different from Maurizio's and the company's early years. They would not try to recapture Gucci's old position. Instead they would place the company in the upper middle of the market—luxury aimed at the masses, closer to Prada and Louis Vuitton. "The idea was fairly simple," De Sole explained. Gucci would be "fashion-forward, high quality, and good value." That means "we would need to be leaders in fashion, deliver products of high quality, and give our customers great value for what they buy from us," he said.[17]

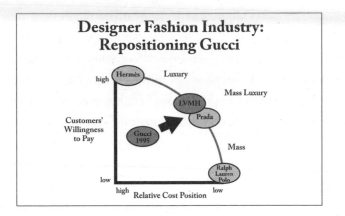

To succeed, Gucci would have to cultivate a new group of customers—younger and more modern—and let go of the wealthy, conservative, older women who had traditionally been its mainstay.[18] The move would be challenging, as Ford explained: The fashion conscious "have a short attention span. They have maybe less brand loyalty than other customers." By contrast, he said, "A classic customer will buy the blue blazer, the cashmere twinset, and replace it when it is worn out. A fashion customer consumes, shops, buys, and disposes of, and then buys again"—which, he noted, made her a very good customer to have,[19] if you can keep her engaged.

"Good value" would also require big trade-offs. Before the family entrepreneurial ventures cheapened the brand, Gucci had built its reputation on delivering the highest quality regardless of cost. By taking apart Hermès's handbags and comparing them with Gucci's, De Sole and his team concluded that their company was still capable of producing goods of high quality, but its cost structure was way out of line. To offer good value, that would have to change. So too would prices.

After rebuilding the entire sourcing network, and lowering Gucci's costs, De Sole ordered price cuts of 30 percent pretty much across the board. Often, EOP executives struggle with that decision. They endorse the principle of good value, but wonder if a reduction of that size is really necessary for a company in such dire straits. It would be a huge hit to an already enfeebled revenue line. "Maybe later," some say, "when things are better. Or by some amount less than thirty percent."

But pricing was key to good value, and important in attracting the customers Gucci wanted. The real downside, De Sole thought, would be *not* cutting prices: Timidity here would have dulled the edge of the strategy.

Ford's first solo collection in October 1994 generated little heat. In his view, it took him a season to "shake off Mello's and Maurizio's influence and call up his own design aesthetic."[20] His second collection, however, in March 1995 brought the company's new purpose to life. Not your mother's Gucci? Not even close. On Tom Ford's runway, there wasn't a single floral scarf, pair of elegant loafers, or classic blazer in sight. Instead, wildly coiffed supermodels sashayed sensuously down the runway in hip-hugging velvet jeans, skinny satin shirts with necklines that plunged to the navel, and car-finish metallic patent boots. *Harper's Bazaar* wrote, "The effortless sexuality of it all had a chill factor that just froze the audience to their seats."[21]

By the next day the showroom was mobbed, and the Gucci brand was reborn.

Consistent with the wishes of Gucci's owners, De Sole took the company public in October 1995. Just three years later, in 1998, the European Business Press federation named Gucci "European Company of the Year" for its economic and financial performance, strategic vision, and management quality.[22]

The financial performance was indeed remarkable. In a report on Gucci in 2001, Credit Suisse dubbed the turnaround "spectacular," noting "a compound annual operating profit expansion of 54 percent on average revenue gains of 36 percent over the five fiscal years to 31 January 2000. Together with earnings acceleration of 80 percent during this period, Gucci has delivered returns on capital of roughly 34 percent on average, well above its 10 percent cost of capital."[23] The media noticed, too. In a cover story, "Style Wars," *Time* magazine opined that "De Sole and Tom Ford . . . pulled off a brand revival so remarkable that any luxury goods firm attempting a turnaround is said to be trying to 'do a Gucci.'"[24] The *Wall Street Journal Europe* declared that Gucci was "the hottest name in luxury goods today for fashion-victims and fund managers alike."[25]

THE BIG QUESTION

Working with Ford, De Sole successfully rebuilt the company based on the purpose he set out in 1995: *fashion-forward, high quality, good value*. But why was De Sole successful and Maurizio not?

Drawing on the story of IKEA, one might guess that De Sole had a compelling purpose and Maurizio did not, or that De Sole's purpose was somehow better than Maurizio's. But it's hard to blame Maurizio's dream for his failure. He had what most observers considered a legitimate purpose: return Gucci to the luxury goods pinnacle it had once occupied. It's an approach—called "going back to the core"—that's often recommended to companies that have lost their way and may profit by returning to their roots and what made them successful in the first place.

Further, Maurizio had captured some smart, hard-nosed investors with his passion. "All the banks loved Maurizio and it was a wonderful vision," said Investcorp's Rick Swanson,[26] yet "there were no consolidated financial statements—at least not at the level we're used to—no definitive central management team, no guarantees. But when he started to spin his story of his vision for Gucci, he charmed other people with his dreams."[27] Even De Sole thought that the big dreams that Maurizio was pursuing were reasonable given the context and resources Maurizio had available at the time.

The difference was not so much in the purpose each chose as in what each man did with the purpose he established. Maurizio's charm blinded his investors to the company's internal disarray and inability to deliver on his promises. De Sole, by contrast, built and executed his strategy in a tightly linked series of actions. Consider how each of these supported the redefined purpose:

Products.

To complement its leather goods, Gucci created a line of original, trendy—and, above all, exciting—ready-to-wear clothing each year, not as the company's mainstay, but as its draw. The idea was that frequent fashion changes in clothing would help the world forget all those counterfeit bags and Gucci toilet paper. "Gucci had to get the message out," De Sole explained, "the real message that Gucci had changed, that it was more exciting, more fashion-forward. We couldn't have gotten that level of excitement around leather bags."[28]

Brand.

One aim of the increased focus on fashion was to propel the company overnight into a new brand identity, generating the kind of excitement that would bring new customers into the stores—where they would be sold not just the latest clothing, but also high-margin handbags and accessories. As a Credit Suisse analyst put it: "The ready-to-wear collection is a showcase for the Gucci identity and lifestyle. It unifies Gucci's various product lines and generates press and editorial coverage, thus serving as a powerful communication vehicle for the brand."[29]

Stores.

To support the new fashion and brand strategies, De Sole and Ford walked through the stores, deciding to ditch Maurizio's clubby "living room," with its heavy cabinets and beveled glass, for a clean, modern look. What changed was more than store décor. As fashion items grew in importance, customer support in the stores was upgraded, too. "Selling ready-to-wear was a more involved sale than selling handbags," De Sole said. "It required a different kind of salesperson."[30] De Sole and Ford paid particular attention to company-operated

stores, which they refurbished and more than doubled in number—
from 63 in 1994 to 143 in 2000.[31]

Marketing.
To spread the word, De Sole doubled advertising spending, and by
1999, advertising and communication constituted 7 percent of sales
revenue. He also made a conscious decision to leverage Tom Ford as
a marketing asset: "Tom is a good-looking man," he explained. "By
making him a force in fashion we could have a face for the company
and accelerate the process of getting the word out."[32] It was not a
decision that was without risk, but De Sole felt that the company
needed the energy a star could bring. (Competitors in time paid the
highest compliment: After Ford became the face and embodiment of
Gucci—both dressing and befriending celebrities like Nicole Kidman,
Gwyneth Paltrow, and Tom and Rita Hanks—Louis Vuitton did the
same with Marc Jacobs and Hermès with Jean Paul Gaultier.[33])

Supply chain.
Unlike the many luxury firms that produced the majority of their
products themselves, Gucci relied on a network of suppliers to
manufacture most of its products. But, when cash was tight and
payments erratic, many suppliers had dropped Gucci. De Sole himself
drove the hilly back roads of Tuscany, where most were located, and
talked to each one. He recaptured the best and let the rest go. For the
best of the best, some twenty-five in all, he provided financial support,
technical training, and advice on improving productivity. In return
he demanded consistent high quality and faster, more dependable
production. To support these efforts, he built an efficient logistics
system and won the support of Italy's infamously tough unions with
the first system of incentive-based bonuses in the business.
As a result, fixed costs went down, while efficiency and the flexibility
to scale production went up—the perfect solution for maintaining
artisanship quality while slashing costs.

Management.

At the top of the organization, De Sole and Ford developed a close partnership. De Sole was responsible for the overall operations of the firm, and Ford was responsible for anything visual—from product design to the creative aspects of advertising, public relations, store design, and corporate communications.[34]

To obtain the management and workforce he needed to support all of this, De Sole replaced Gucci's traditional family-based management system, racked by politics and infighting, with one that was merit based and performance focused. After the company sold stock to the public, managers were rewarded with stock options, a tool unavailable to many of Gucci's privately held competitors. "I get all the best people," De Sole said at the time. "People like working at Gucci. And we pay them better, too."[35]

In effect, everything De Sole did in design, product lineup, pricing, marketing, distribution, manufacturing, logistics, organizational culture, and management was tied tightly to purpose. It was all coordinated, internally consistent, and interlocking, a system of resources and activities that worked together and reinforced each other, all aimed at producing products that were fashion-forward, high quality, and good value.

THE BIG IDEA

The essential difference between Maurizio Gucci and De Sole is that a great purpose is not a great strategy. A great strategy is more than an aspiration, more than a dream: It's a *system of value creation, a set of mutually reinforcing parts*. Anchored by a compelling purpose, it tells you where a company will play, how it will play, and what it will accomplish.

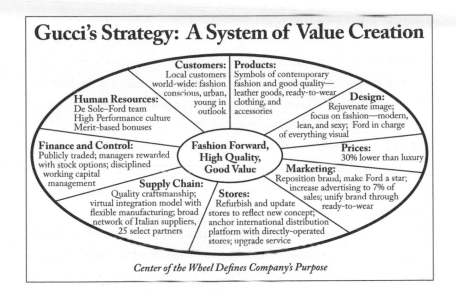

Gucci's Strategy: A System of Value Creation

Customers:
Local customers world-wide: fashion conscious, urban, young in outlook

Products:
Symbols of contemporary fashion and good quality—leather goods, ready-to-wear clothing, and accessories

Design:
Rejuvenate image; focus on fashion—modern, lean, and sexy; Ford in charge of everything visual

Human Resources:
De Sole–Ford team
High Performance culture
Merit-based bonuses

Finance and Control:
Publicly traded; managers rewarded with stock options; disciplined working capital management

Prices:
30% lower than luxury

Fashion Forward, High Quality, Good Value

Marketing:
Reposition brand; make Ford a star; increase advertising to 7% of sales; unify brand through ready-to-wear

Supply Chain:
Quality craftsmanship; virtual integration model with flexible manufacturing; broad network of Italian suppliers, 25 select partners

Stores:
Refurbish and update stores to reflect new concept; anchor international distribution platform with directly-operated stores; upgrade service

Center of the Wheel Defines Company's Purpose

It is easy to see the beauty of such a system once it's constructed—but constructing isn't always an easy or a beautiful process. The decisions embedded in such systems are often gutsy choices. For every moving part in the Gucci universe, De Sole had to decide what he believed was the choice that would specifically advance the purpose of the firm. This was strictly binary management: Either the particular component advanced the purpose of fashion-forwardness, high quality, and good value, or it was rebuilt. Strategists call such choices "identity-conferring commitments"—they reflect what an organization stands for. They are the choices that are central to what a firm is or wants to be. In De Sole's case, many of these choices were spontaneous, but they flowed from a clear understanding of what the firm was trying to accomplish.

Too many leaders, unwilling to give up any possible advantage, take the easy route and dodge or defer the tough decisions: "Let's not give up our traditional customers while we bring the new ones along." Not so with De Sole. He was willing to make trade-offs.[36] Each choice he made threatened a loss even as it promised a gain—focusing on new customers, lowering prices, letting a lot of suppliers go. But, with each decision, he was asserting that Gucci was going to be one thing and not another, a formidable responsibility made more difficult when dealing with a very sick company.

Yet the crisis also made some things easier because all the decisions were more urgent. "When a company has problems, you have to move forward," De Sole said. "The crisis really helped us out. You're much more likely to make a lot of changes when things are bad. When you are trying to resurrect a company, you have to move forward. You can't keep looking back. You can't give people a chance to make excuses. You have to take responsibility."[37]

Systems like the one De Sole put in place answer the question: How are you going to deliver on your promise? They are the critical first steps in translating an idea into a strategy and paving the way for its realization. De Sole's finely tuned, tailor-made system made it possible for him to carry out his purpose. Maurizio didn't have such a system—he had a lot of shoot-from-the-hip grand actions that didn't work in concert; inwardly focused, he grew increasingly out of sync with the reality in which he was operating. Unlike De Sole with fashion, he had no device, other than his lavish spending, to change people's perceptions or boost their willingness to pay. He had no way to cover the firm's increasing costs. He had few, if any, scarce resources to undergird his strategy and stave off competition.

The role of scarcity is particularly easy to overlook in a strategy. But without it a firm may have an internally consistent system built around an interesting innovative idea, only to see it quickly imitated at the first signs of success. Warren Buffett refers to this kind of scarcity as an "economic moat," a barrier that keeps other competition away. The bigger and deeper the moat, the more attractive he finds the company as an investment. For some companies, that moat might be physically unique assets, such as oil and gas properties, mineral rights, real estate locations, or patents. Large companies may have such massive scale that others can't surpass them. (Think Wal-Mart or Microsoft.) Others may have intangible resources, such as brands, that are built over time and difficult to duplicate. (For instance, an adult's long-lived associations with the Disney brand or an athlete's feelings about Gatorade.) Other distinctive components may be capabilities or routines that are just too complex for others to disentangle or reconstruct.

When I ask EOP executives which of these kinds of resources tend to shore up most outstanding strategies, they're likely to pick the first two—physically unique assets or those relating to huge economic scale. But, in fact, the resources that are particularly valuable in most strategies are the last two: intangible resources such as brands and corporate reputations, and complex organizational capabilities and routines that are vital to a firm's distinctiveness yet relatively scarce and difficult to imitate. De Sole's Gucci boasts both: the powerful intangible of the restored Gucci brand, and a high-performance culture, design capability, network of skilled suppliers, and international distribution platform anchored by company-run stores. All of these are valuable in their own right, and boosted Gucci's competitiveness.

Knitting all these individual components together and driving them toward a compelling purpose is the finely honed system of value creation. When they exist, such systems themselves are among a firm's most important resources. In the best of cases, they have all the qualities that make a resource valuable: They are important to competitive advantage; they are uniquely tailored and in short supply; and they are difficult to imitate because of their complexity and the way they develop over time.

One revealing measure of the value De Sole created with his system—not only for the Gucci brand, but also as a platform for expansion—was a takeover attempt. In the mid-1990s, when Investcorp was trying to sell Gucci, Bernard Arnault, head of LVMH (Louis Vuitton Moët Hennessy), was unwilling to pay just $400 million for the company. But in 1999, LVMH began buying shares in Gucci, and Arnault reportedly offered between $8 billion and $9 billion for total control of the firm, a twentyfold increase in five years.

De Sole fought back and eventually found a white knight in Pinault Printemps Redoute (later known as PPR), which paid $3 billion for 40 percent of the company in 1999 and agreed to infuse additional money for acquisitions and expansions. In the bidding war, Gucci's business model—its system of value creation—was arguably the asset valued most. "I like building things," said François Pinault, PPR's founder. "This is the chance to create a global group."[38] Gucci's system, so critical to its own competitive advantage, could serve as a platform for a multibusiness company, enabling PPR to add value to a host of similar businesses.

STARS AND STRATEGY

But what about the wonderful guys from Gucci? Aren't *they* the company's most valuable resource? They're the ones who turned Gucci around. They're the ones who put the system in place.

EOPers always give De Sole and Ford credit for much of Gucci's success, and well they should. There is no doubt that De Sole and Ford individually and as a team created enormous amounts of value for the firm. But to identify a *company's* valuable resources, one has to look farther than individuals, no matter how talented. A company's story may start with key people or star players, but there has to be a lot more to it. When PPR invested in the company, the all-star De Sole–Ford team was no doubt part of the attraction—but perhaps not as much as you would think. When the company acquired Gucci's remaining outstanding shares in 2004, making it a wholly owned subsidiary, De Sole and Ford asked for "ironclad guarantees for their managerial freedom" and a pledge to maintain several independent directors on Gucci's supervisory board. Though PPR paid them handsomely—making De Sole an offer that was "above his expectations," according to the *Wall Street Journal*—it refused to guarantee them the independence they wanted.[39] The two men, who had made many millions of dollars from their Gucci stock, left the company shortly thereafter.

There was an outcry from observers who, like the EOPers, were shocked and dismayed by the departure. But Gucci didn't collapse; in fact, since then the firm has had some resoundingly strong periods of performance, and some weaker ones as well. Would Gucci's path have been brighter if De Sole and Ford had stayed? Many argue that it would have been. But, more than anything, the firm's ability to go on without them is testament to the value of what they built.

THE EDGE

In an interview, I asked De Sole to comment on what he considered his most important achievement at Gucci. His answer:

We made fashion a real business. We were tougher. We were more competitive. We relaunched the company but we also helped to change the universe of fashion. It used to be dominated by small, private, family-run companies that often weren't profitable. It took us several years to get there, but we showed that you could make a lot of money in fashion.[40]

De Sole and Ford didn't do that through a few grand gestures. They did it through a thorough understanding of the industry, a coherent idea of what they wanted Gucci to be, and a frenetic but disciplined march through every activity that needed to be rebuilt and brought into line. "Like everything in life," De Sole said, "it was a lot of little things. We were very aggressive in establishing priorities, and needed to act decisively, quickly."

Many people believe a strategist's primary job is thinking. It isn't. The number-one job is setting an agenda and putting in place the organization to carry it out. "Some companies have great strategies and do a lot of talking," said De Sole, "but they don't get it done. I follow through. I call my managers all the time to make sure they have executed what they said they would do."[41]

Every year, early in the term, someone in class always wants to engage the group in a discussion about what's more important: strategy or execution? In my view, it's a false dichotomy, a wrongheaded debate that they themselves have to resolve, and I let them have their go at it. I always bring that discussion up again at the end of the Gucci case, asking, "What here is strategy?" "What is execution?" "Where does one end and the other begin?" Often there isn't a clear answer—and maybe that's as it should be. What could be more desirable than a well-conceived strategy that flows without a ripple into execution?

Thinking of strategy as a *system of value creation*, rich in organizational detail and driven by purpose, underscores the point. It's the bridge between lofty ideas and action. But while it's easy to see it in companies like Gucci or IKEA, when all the details are laid out in front of you, I know from working with thousands of organizations just how rare it is to find a carefully honed system that really delivers.

The problems often begin right at the start. If leaders lack a clear idea about what they want their businesses to be, they cannot build coherent systems of value creation because they don't know what they should be designed to do exactly or how their success should be measured. That leaves them to fiddle at the margins of success with generically good practices such as "state of the art" sales management approaches or Total Quality Management.[42] These may be helpful, but they're not what will help you find an edge and live on it.

You and every leader of a company must ask yourself whether your strategy is a real system of value creation—a clearly defined purpose tightly backed by a set of mutually reinforcing parts.

If not, it's time to build one. That's the job to be tackled next.

6

OWN YOUR STRATEGY

IT'S YOUR TURN.

You've studied the successes and setbacks of Masco, IKEA, and Gucci. You know that every business, every organization, needs a strategy. You understand the importance of a meaningful purpose and a tightly aligned system of value creation. Now it's time to look at your own company. What's your strategy?

When I put this question to the entrepreneurs and presidents toward the end of our program, many of them nod confidently. By this point we have been talking about strategy for a long time and they have a good grasp of the principles. And they've repeatedly shown their ability to identify the strengths and weaknesses in the strategies of well-known and celebrated firms—at a safe distance.

But when I press them to describe their own strategies, many struggle. Beyond somewhat sweeping statements, they often have trouble articulating what their businesses actually do or what sets them apart. The ideas come out vague; the statements they write down tend to be generic and uninspired.

It's a struggle because analyzing yourself is always harder than analyzing someone else. The cool objectivity and clarity you enjoy as a spectator often gives way to uncertainty and doubt when you start to confront the reality of your own situation.

While the intense class work exposes EOPers to the tools of strategy, for many there is a chasm between their understanding of how strategy works and truly being strategists—like the difference between war games and war, between reading about how to swim and actually swimming.

*"I've never actually stormed a castle, but I've taken
a bunch of siege-management courses."*

The reality is that it can be hard to put strategic thinking to work in one's own business. Managers often start off on the wrong foot, failing to think carefully about purpose, or they don't take the process far enough to see how all the activities in their businesses support (or don't support) their intended direction. Studying other companies' dilemmas and other managers' triumphs is a good start, but it's not enough. To develop into a successful strategist you must live the experience. You must wrestle with the specific purpose of your company, find the differences that matter, define your system of value creation, and pull it all together into a compelling strategy.

There's only one way to begin effectively: write all these things down.

Writing imposes a discipline that no amount of talking can match: It gives structure to your thinking. It forces you to define in carefully considered words what your business exists to do and how each part of it contributes to the effort. Once that's laid out, you can analyze why the whole thing works or doesn't and what could make it stronger.

This is not a casual exercise: You will find yourself visiting and revisiting your work. A winning strategy doesn't just rise up out of your keyboard in an afternoon or emerge from a weekend retreat with your team. Rather, for most leaders, it comes into focus over time, as you analyze and reflect on your business and work through each step of the process.[1]

In addition to building your strategic skills, the experience helps you to clarify your strategy for all of your stakeholders. Many companies never accomplish this, instead offering up grand statements or euphemisms that convey very little about the business itself or its particular reason for being. As we discussed this in class one day, one of the EOPers told the group that before coming to campus he had looked up the websites for all 170-plus companies that would be represented in the program. What he found often wasn't impressive. Very few, he reported, gave him a credible sense of what the company was really about—what made it special, or why he should care about it.

Other hands went up; those people had done the same thing and come to the same conclusion. There were a lot of sober faces around the room as the message sank in.

The internal costs of unclear strategies are, arguably, even greater. As information technology consultant James Champy notes, "few companies are explicit about the future: in what markets they will operate, how large and quickly can they grow, how will they differentiate. . . ." This vagueness, he said, leaves employees feeling completely in the dark, unable to accurately anticipate the firm's future needs or do their jobs well. Instead, they must resort to reading the tea leaves, trying to guess the strategy by analyzing management's actions.[2]

A clearly defined strategy steers the company, providing a compass for where you want to go. It makes you a better communicator, giving you the words to articulate what you are doing and why. Your customers and investors will understand you better. Your employees won't have to guess what you're up to and they will know how their work fits into the whole and what will be expected of them.

In the EOP program, this strategy development process has led to dramatic insights: Some executives come to the painful conclusion that they need to jettison a product line or sell a whole business; others uncover missed opportunities or stake out new positions. Three cases in brief:

Dr. Richard Ajayi, the head of The Bridge Clinic, Nigeria's first focused in-vitro fertilization clinic, took enormous pride in its high quality standards and differentiated service. But, looking closely at his experience, he realized that customers who could afford the company's prices often went overseas for care, while those in the low to middle end of the market didn't understand the value of the science involved and couldn't pay the premium price. In response, Ajayi reduced all costs unrelated to patient outcomes, explicitly benchmarked the clinic's outcomes on the highest international standards, and recast it as high quality but affordable health care with the motto: "We are within your reach, make the decision and grasp." The repositioning enabled the clinic to meet the needs of thousands of patients and generated unprecedented growth.

Geoff Piceu's grandfather founded United Paint and Chemical in 1953, and the company grew into a solid player in the automotive coatings industry. But in the early 2000s, competition in the industry was cutthroat. The younger Piceu, who had taken over by then, described the competitive landscape as "a disaster you wouldn't want to hear about," and Michigan-based United was struggling to make a profit. Piceu concluded that his best chance for survival was to become the low-cost producer. Having learned that innovation had a short shelf-life in automotive coatings — it gets commoditized quickly—he abandoned the expensive basic research that was traditional in the industry, choosing instead to adopt a "second-to-market" approach by acquiring innovation and being a fast follower. He also reshaped operations into a paragon of lean manufacturing. The new strategy roughly doubled United's productivity relative to competitors and led to double-digit sales growth.

Eugene Marchese, the founder of an Australian architecture firm, was considering expansion to other residential segments and geographies in his home country. At the time, however, it was not yet clear what the firm's unique advantage would be in those new markets. Instead, he decided to expand to 2nd Tier cities overseas where he could leverage the firm's award-winning designs for urban-condominiums and share personnel and other resources across time zones. Today, Marchese Partners has offices in cities ranging from Sydney to San Francisco to Guangzhou, and provides its innovative design services and commercial sensitivity to leading developers anywhere in the world.

In all these cases, the work began by revisiting the organization's purpose, a good place to start the examination of your own business.

STATE YOUR PURPOSE

As we discussed in chapter 4, your company's purpose describes the unique value your firm brings to the world. It's the throbbing heartbeat of your strategy—the grand pronouncement of who you are and why you matter. It should be specific and easy to grasp because the rest of your strategy flows from and supports this beginning.

Too often I see companies describe their purpose as something like,

The best company in XYZ industry, specializing in satisfied customers, or *Our nonprofit is committed to improving the quality of life in our community.* Or this:

> *We will provide branded products and services of superior quality and value that improve the lives of the world's consumers, now and for generations to come. As a result, consumers will reward us with leadership sales, profit and value creation, allowing our people, our shareholders, and the communities in which we live and work to prosper.[3]*

How could you even guess that the last one is from Procter & Gamble, the giant consumer products company?

Contrast that with some other companies:

> _____: *To bring inspiration and innovation to every athlete in the world.[4]*

> _____ *is built upon finding ways to do online search better and faster in an increasing number of new places and in ever more efficient ways.[5]*

And this:

> *The _____Group is the only manufacturer of automobiles and motorcycles worldwide that concentrates entirely on premium standards and outstanding quality for all its brands and across all relevant segments.[6]*

Do you recognize Nike, Google, and BMW? They each have a grasp on why they exist and who they are.

What is your company's purpose? Is it something everyone in your company knows?

Sometimes a slogan can begin to capture the purpose—or at least start the discussion—if it gets to the firm's unique added value. EOPer H. Kerr Taylor, founder of a Houston real estate firm called AmREIT, told me where he got the initial idea for his company. As a young man visiting Florence, Italy, during a post-graduation tour of Europe, he was impressed by the big, beautiful, multipurpose buildings on a plaza that housed shops and offices on the ground floor, and apartments above. He asked an older gentleman sitting next to him at a café who the owners were. "These buildings are owned by some of the wealthiest families of Italy," the man told him, explaining that they were rarely, if ever, sold. "That is how you pass wealth down from generation to generation."

After earning an MBA and a law degree and returning home to Houston, Taylor set out to try to build a portfolio like the ones that supported those wealthy Italian families. Because his nascent company was short on capital, he initially focused on buying and leasing back great corner properties with one tenant, such as bank branches or restaurants. Eventually he moved up to entire shopping centers, all situated on prime corners. Along the way his company latched on to a slogan that described its work: the "Irreplaceable Corner" Company. It was a powerful moniker: "When people saw that on our sign, it stuck with them," he said.

At the time Taylor joined EOP, his business had hit a plateau after more than two decades of growth. As he began to formulate a strategy statement, he and his executive team experimented with different ways to tell their story. This seemingly simple exercise led to major revelations about the nature of the business, and its difference that matters. When they put together a chart that mapped their properties and those of their top peers (over 800 properties in all), it was clear that AmREIT, though relatively small compared with industry giants, was a leader in focusing on real estate near high numbers of affluent households, a position that was particularly attractive to big-money investors. Using 2015 demographic projections, the gap between them and their peers grew even larger. Only one other major real estate company even came close.

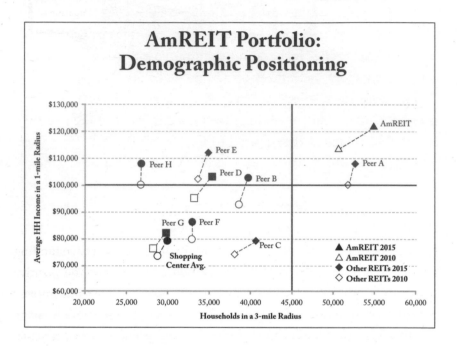

As Kerr and his team studied the chart and chewed on the language in their strategy, they began to ask what "The Irreplaceable Corner" really meant. Their efforts to nail down the firm's purpose, and to ease its implementation, drove them much deeper into defining the kind of properties the company would buy, where they would be located, and how they would be chosen. This yielded highly specific criteria: the corners would be near large numbers of households, especially affluent ones; near high-traffic roads, and in areas with dense daytime and nighttime populations.

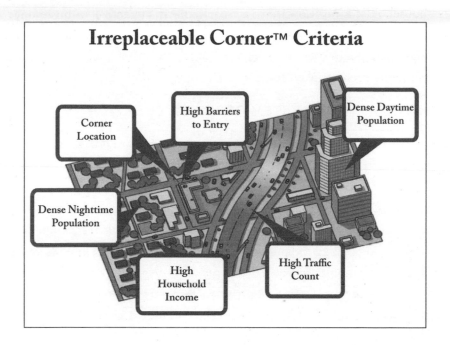

Irreplaceable Corner™ Criteria

Corner Location

High Barriers to Entry

Dense Daytime Population

Dense Nighttime Population

High Household Income

High Traffic Count

Crystallizing the company's purpose led to a better understanding of what made its approach different and effective. It created a positive feedback loop. Not only did the new depth of detail help the company improve its operations, Taylor says, it also helped fit the firm's strategy to its purpose, tell AmREIT's story to employees and potential tenants, and win the attention of institutional investors who tend to overlook a company of AmREIT's size.

To Taylor's surprise, a good part of the initial process was about words. "I didn't understand how important language was, trying to get the words correctly so you could communicate to others and, in the process, really communicate to yourself in a clear way," he says.

AmREIT's work fits the definition of corporate purpose that John Browne, former CEO of British Petroleum, spelled out in an interview with the *Harvard Business Review*: "Our purpose is who we are and what makes us distinctive. It's what we as a company exist to achieve. . . ." As you work to identify and define the purpose for your own company, don't stop with your first idea, but like Taylor, refine and clarify. The more precisely you can express it, the better the anchor it will become for developing your strategy—and, quite possibly, the more new insights you will gain into your business.

DEVELOP YOUR SYSTEM OF VALUE CREATION

By now you know that a company's purpose is just a beginning. As discussed in chapter 5, it gives you the right to play, and puts you in the game. But it doesn't mean you have the right to *win*. Just as De Sole made sure that each component of the Gucci enterprise—design, sourcing, stores, products, pricing, and so on—aligned with the company's purpose, so must all of your activities and resources work in concert to support your own purpose.

You need to pinpoint who the customer is early in the process. But which customer? It's not always the end user. Laura Young joined Leegin, the predecessor company of Brighton Collectibles, in 1991, when it was primarily a seller of men's belts, and the owner, Jerry Kohl, wanted to expand into ladies' leather goods. Since then, the company has added handbags, wallets, jewelry, and shoes, creating a significant niche as a boutique specializing in women's moderately priced accessories. But even now, with over $350 million in annual sales, Brighton remains an unconventional company. Still owned fully by Kohl, there is no board of directors, no organization chart, and few formal titles. Kohl and Young work together as partners managing the company.

When Young began to define the strategy for Brighton, she struggled with where the company's focus should be. The question of who the customer was loomed large: Was it the end consumer, the women who snapped up the matching pieces and shared their finds with their friends, in what Young calls "Girlfriend Marketing"? Was it the owners of the several thousand largely family-owned specialty boutiques that carried Brighton's accessories or the sales associates in those boutiques and in Brighton's company-owned stores? Or, was it the roughly one hundred dedicated sales representatives who called on all those stores?

Each group mattered, and each played a role in Brighton's unique approach to the market. Ultimately, Young decided that the people who sell its products—the company's sales representatives and the stores' owners and sales associates—were its customers because they were the ones whose dedication could most influence the consumer's purchase decision. Keeping them happy, and their work profitable, was key to Brighton's own health.

So how does Young align Brighton's operations—its system of value creation—behind these salespeople?

To keep merchandise fresh and interesting for them, the company makes "a little bit of a lot of things," rather than huge quantities of a few items. That means the retailers can vary the choices and give the women who buy its products a lot of different options to choose from. Brighton also keeps the sales associates engaged with a steady flow of creative motivational events, seminars, and other opportunities to learn about the brand. For nearly two decades, Young and Kohl have taken hundreds of store operators and employees on trips to Los Angeles, Hong Kong, China, Taiwan, and Italy where they tour factories, eat meals together, and have continuous time for collaboration.

"We do things differently from other companies in our industry," says Young. "We make sure we reach the sales associates who are the ones interacting everyday with customers. There is a real passion to what we do. A real spirit for the brand." Fostering that spirit is crucial, she continues. "Without passion the sales associates can't do what they need to do in their stores. They have to have a point of difference. The customer has to have a good experience because she has so many other options." These days those options include the Internet. And—all retailers take note—Brighton's motivated sales associates provide something you can't get online. "The customer needs to feel good every time she goes into the store," says Young. "She needs to have a great shopping experience, and a real personal and warm connection with the sales associate who is helping her."

Importantly, Brighton also protects the boutiques by refusing to sell to big department stores such as Macy's, Dillard's, and Neiman Marcus. They have come courting, but Young has turned them all away, sometimes sending flowers or cookies with her sincere apologies that she won't do business with them.

In return, Brighton makes an unusual demand of its retailers: It requires them to sell at a minimum resale price in order to protect the integrity of the brand so that customers know they are being treated fairly no matter where they shop for Brighton. The pricing policy also allows for sufficient margins for retailers so that they can provide the generous customer service, in-store ambience, and shopping amenities that are synonymous with the Brighton brand.[7] It is so committed to this approach that when tiny Kay's Kloset in suburban Dallas insisted on discounting the line and took Brighton to court, the company fought back. After the U.S. Court of Appeals for the Fifth Circuit ruled in Kay's favor, citing decades of precedents, the company appealed to the U.S. Supreme Court, which sided with Brighton's point of view.

In so doing, Brighton changed the landscape of American retailing: The decision overturned a ninety-six-year-old piece of the Sherman Antitrust Act and told courts that manufacturers and distributors sometimes could, in fact, insist on minimum prices, so long as the effects of such policies, as in Brighton's case, are pro-competitive.[8] Although the company has grown considerably since then and now includes more than 160 company-owned Brighton Collectibles stores, maintaining minimum retail prices on its goods remains a cornerstone of its strategy.

To begin to capture these decisions and the role they play in Brighton's system of value creation, or what Young likes to call "the secret sauce," we could make a list of the company's various operations and how they work in concert to support the company's purpose. For instance, the trips with boutique owners and the full-price policy are key parts of the company's marketing efforts. The product range, sales and distribution channels are part of the system too, as are the company's information technology systems, operations, human resources, and finance functions. They all support the same goals with activities that are consistent and specific to Brighton's approach.

THE STRATEGY WHEEL

To visualize and record how a system of value creation backs up a firm's purpose, I use a time-honored approach that has come to be known as a "strategy wheel."

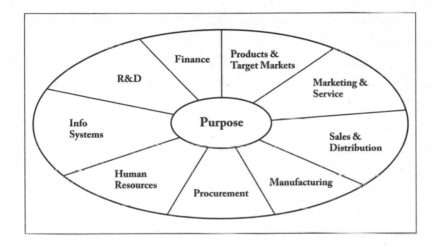

As we saw in the Gucci case in chapter 5, the strategy wheel provides a picture of *how* you will win. The purpose in the center says why you exist—what you do differently or better than others—and the unique configuration of activities and resources around the rim shows what will enable you to deliver on that promise. Brighton's strategy does this well.

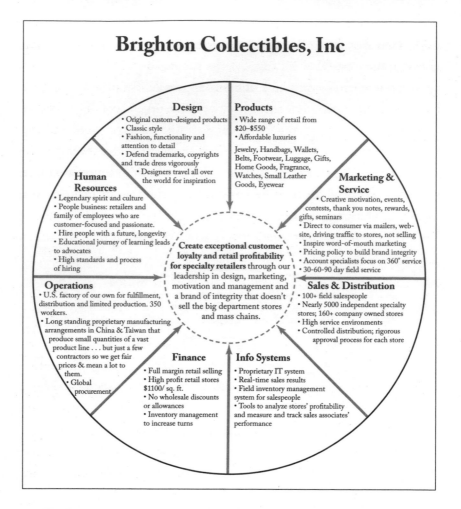

Brighton Collectibles, Inc

Design
- Original custom-designed products
- Classic style
- Fashion, functionality and attention to detail
- Defend trademarks, copyrights and trade dress vigorously
- Designers travel all over the world for inspiration

Products
- Wide range of retail from $20–$550
- Affordable luxuries

Jewelry, Handbags, Wallets, Belts, Footwear, Luggage, Gifts, Home Goods, Fragrance, Watches, Small Leather Goods, Eyewear

Human Resources
- Legendary spirit and culture
- People business: retailers and family of employees who are customer-focused and passionate.
- Hire people with a future, longevity
- Educational journey of learning leads to advocates
- High standards and process of hiring

Marketing & Service
- Creative motivation, events, contests, thank you notes, rewards, gifts, seminars
- Direct to consumer via mailers, web-site, driving traffic to stores, not selling
- Inspire word-of-mouth marketing
- Pricing policy to build brand integrity
- Account specialists focus on 360° service
- 30-60-90 day field service

Operations
- U.S. factory of our own for fulfillment, distribution and limited production. 350 workers.
- Long standing proprietary manufacturing arrangements in China & Taiwan that produce small quantities of a vast product line . . . but just a few contractors so we get fair prices & mean a lot to them.
- Global procurement

Create exceptional customer loyalty and retail profitability for specialty retailers through our leadership in design, marketing, motivation and management and a brand of integrity that doesn't sell the big department stores and mass chains.

Sales & Distribution
- 100+ field salespeople
- Nearly 5000 independent specialty stores; 160+ company owned stores
- High service environments
- Controlled distribution; rigorous approval process for each store

Finance
- Full margin retail selling
- High profit retail stores $1100/ sq. ft.
- No wholesale discounts or allowances
- Inventory management to increase turns

Info Systems
- Proprietary IT system
- Real-time sales results
- Field inventory management system for salespeople
- Tools to analyze stores' profitability and measure and track sales associates' performance

Each system of value creation, and thus each strategy wheel, will be different, because every organization has its own purpose and unique set of activities that drive that purpose. Even the headings around the rim will differ across firms—for example, while R&D will be important in one firm, in another it wouldn't even appear on the wheel.

The point of this work isn't about "checking boxes" or "getting all the way around the wheel." It's about spending time thinking about your business and challenging yourself to see what's really there—and even more, envisioning what could be there. Just penciling in what you do in finance, human resources, R&D, or any other function in a mechanical way isn't likely to be helpful; identifying a bunch of plain-vanilla activities around a plain-vanilla purpose won't leave you any better off than you are today.

Rather, when it works best, the process is a lot like putting together a jigsaw puzzle. Each piece must work with the others, coming together to create a picture of what your business can be. The real work and the real payoff come when you're assertive, when you push the envelope and ask: What would winning really take? How could this element do more for us? What could we do differently if we narrowed our focus to one type of target customer? Gradually, as you define and refine, you should begin to identify not just what you do better and worse than the other guy, but what aspects of your company—from your customer base to what you do for them—make you *different*, and truly give you an edge, or could do so.

As Philippine entrepreneur Amable "Miguel" Aguiluz IX developed his strategy wheel, he began to see his business in a holistic way. In 2002, Aguiluz started Ink for Less to provide a cheaper alternative to OEM printer cartridges—sorely needed in a country with per-capita income of roughly $2,600 at the time. Today the company sells a vast variety of ink and toner cartridges, toners, do-it-yourself refill kits, continuous feed systems, and related products and services. The dominant supplier in the Philippines, Ink for Less has more than 600 outlets and an expanding franchise operation.

At the center of Aguiluz's strategy wheel is this well-crafted and clear purpose: "Readily available and reliable 100% quality ink refills and service at competitive prices." Building the system around it led him to reconsider how every element of the business could contribute to the whole. Pricing, of course, is crucial. His customers currently might pay $6 to $8 to refill a $25 or $30 cartridge or about $16 to refill a $75 toner cartridge. So Aguiluz pays special attention to elements, such as logistics, that affect his costs. His people scour the region for quality inks at good prices. "When I started, I was buying bottles of ink," he says. "Now I am buying fifteen tons of ink per month. That shows you the power of volume I can command with my suppliers." Sales costs are important, too; Aguiluz works hard to keep them in the single digits. This discipline around costs has given him the flexibility to drive his prices lower to respond aggressively to competitive threats. When a franchisee of an Australian chain came into his market, for example, he was able to respond by dramatically lowering his prices at nearby stores.

Refilling ink cartridges isn't an especially high-tech operation. Nevertheless, Aguiluz realized that research and development had to be a cornerstone of his strategy. Without it he wouldn't be able to stand up to the printer manufacturers, or contend with mom-and-pop competitors, who might charge less than he does. For example, printer manufacturers try to foil ink refillers by continually redesigning cartridges and changing where they hide the entry holes. In response, Aguiluz's R&D crew buys every single printer and every single cartridge as it comes to market so they can reverse-engineer them and figure out how they work. When printer makers added a chip that shuts down the printer if the cartridge isn't new, his R&D people worked with their suppliers around Asia to learn how to add a counter-chip so that the refilled cartridge would work. These efforts not only keep Ink for Less in business, they enable it to provide better service than less sophisticated players. Bulletins and videos are sent regularly to the stores, alerting outlet managers and technicians to new cartridges and new processes, so that nothing customers bring in will stump them.

Over time, Aguiluz and his staff have built out cascading sets of activities for every spoke on the wheel (see, for example, Human Resources and Training). They revisit them frequently to make changes that help Ink for Less maintain or increase its lead in the market. Aguiluz often returns to the strategy wheel on his own— sometimes spending a full day working through the implications of a particular action, such as a pricing change, going from spoke to spoke to see what adjustments need to be made to keep the wheel in alignment.

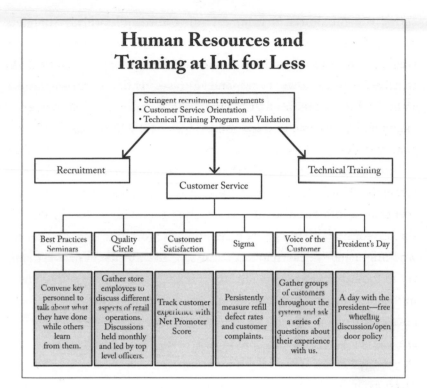

His rigor pays off. In 2008, the Philippines Junior Chamber International named Aguiluz its "Creative Young Entrepreneur" of the year. Over the last nine years, Ink for Less's sales have grown at an average annual rate of 15 percent, and profits have grown even faster. But Ink for Less is not only capturing value for itself; it is making its customers better off than they would have been if the firm weren't there.

REALITY CHECK

You will likely have to make a number of assumptions in building your wheel. Check them carefully! People in all professions go astray because they're operating on untested assumptions. In strategy, these are often a recipe for disaster. Be ruthless in challenging what you *think* you know.

It's particularly easy to make this mistake when it comes to the linkage between your stated purpose and your system of value creation—is it really designed to do what you say, and is it working? Too often, I've seen executives claim their companies are high-end, differentiated companies seeking to make a difference by offering customers not lower prices, but better-than-average goods. They have everything lined up—except customers who share that view and are willing to pay a premium for their products or services. Remember how Maurizio Gucci staked the company's future on top-of-the-line products that customers stayed away from in droves? The linkage simply wasn't there.

To assess whether what you are doing is working, you need to look for the data and the facts, and not just rely on intuition. What evidence do you have that you are the low-cost provider or the premium producer you say you are? Where, exactly, in the process do you add value? Can you support that view with facts—internal process measures of key performance drivers, and outcome measures like sales results, profit margins, market share, or return on investment?

Consider how Walter de Mattos does this. A longtime Brazilian journalist, he founded Lance! Sports Group in 1997 to capture his fellow sports fans' obsession with their favorite soccer teams. Since then it has grown from a daily sports newspaper in two cities to five more editions plus magazine, television, mobile, and Web versions that give Lance! a national platform and make it the largest sports news organization and leading authority in Brazil.

Embedded in de Mattos's strategy wheel is a self-reinforcing system of elements: Multitask journalists provide unique content to a variety of platforms, driving readership. Large readership, in turn, brings in regional and national advertisers. Both the depth and breadth of soccer coverage and the size of the circulation serve as barriers to entry, making it harder for competitors to make inroads. To focus resources on his strengths and manage costs, he outsources distribution of the print newspaper and works with an external design firm.

De Mattos assesses whether the individual parts of the system are working, and in sync, by looking at specific, tangible results: estimated readers per week (2.3 million in 2011); unique website visitors (750,000 a day, some of whom check the site more than once); and cost per story (lower than a pure television producer or newspaper publisher because content is shared across the Web, print, and video outlets). Over the last five years, these collectively gave Lance! one of the highest rates of growth and return on investment among Brazilian media companies.

What do your metrics tell you about your strategy? Are they consistent with your rhetoric? Do they show that you are winning with your plan?

PULLING IT ALL TOGETHER

After you've identified your purpose, aligned your activities and resources, and tested the results—all internal working steps—you are ready to summarize your strategy in a statement you can use to communicate that commitment both inside and outside your firm. You don't need to use formal language or any particular format; the most important goal is conveying your unique aspects and advantages with specific and engaging words.

Here are three examples of memorable strategy statements from well-known organizations. Can you tell who they are?

A hotelier:

_____ is dedicated to perfecting the travel experience through continuous innovation and the highest standards of hospitality. From elegant surroundings of the finest quality, to caring, highly personalized 24-hour service, _____ embodies a true home away from home for those who know and appreciate the best. The deeply instilled _____ culture is personified in its employees—people who share a single focus and are inspired to offer great service.

*Founded in 1960, _____ has followed a targeted course
of expansion, opening hotels in major city centres and desirable
resort destinations around the world. Currently with 75 hotels
in 31 countries, and more than 31 properties under development,
_____ will continue to lead the hospitality industry with
innovative enhancements, making business travel easier and leisure
travel more rewarding.*[9]

A magazine:

*Edited in London since 1843, _____ is a weekly international
news and business publication, offering clear reporting, commentary
and analysis on world current affairs, business, finance, science
and technology, culture, society, media and the arts. As noted on its
contents page, _____'s goal is to "take part in a severe contest
between intelligence, which presses forward, and an unworthy,
timid ignorance obstructing our progress." Printed in five countries,
worldwide circulation is now over one million, and _____ is
read by more of the world's political and business leaders than any
other magazine.*[10]

An accompanying document describes its editorial policy, including its fierce commitment to independence and its practice of being
written anonymously, with no bylines, to make it a paper "whose collective voice and personality matter more than the identities of individual journalists."

A nonprofit:

*_____ is an international medical humanitarian organization
created by doctors and journalists. . . . Today, _____ provides
independent, impartial assistance in more than 60 countries*

to people whose survival is threatened by violence, neglect,
or catastrophe, primarily due to armed conflict, epidemics,
malnutrition, exclusion from health care, or natural disasters. . . .
_____ also reserves the right to speak out to bring attention to
neglected crises, challenge inadequacies or abuse of the aid system,
and to advocate for improved medical treatments and protocols.[11]

You probably recognize the Four Seasons Resorts, the *Economist*, and Doctors Without Borders from language that is closely linked with them, like "highest standards of hospitality," "contest between intelligence and ignorance," and "independent, impartial assistance." Beyond that, though, are prescriptive elements that define their advantages, describe what they stand for, and tell you something important about how that work will be done.

There are plenty of hotels around, for instance, but Four Seasons defines its service culture as a unique attribute that gives it a strategic difference. There are plenty of magazines as well, but many are languishing while the *Economist*, with its fierce independence, incisive commentary, and timely reporting, gains ground. The Doctors Without Borders statement makes clear that the Nobel Peace Prize–winning organization doesn't just provide impartial medical assistance; it also advocates for change.

To break the process down further, a good strategy statement articulates a company's purpose, its means of competition, and its unique advantages by answering the most basic questions about what a company does and how it does it:

• Who we serve
• With what sort of products or services
• What we do that's different or better
• What enables us to do that

And it has these qualities:

- It is reasonably short and parsimonious.
- It is specific.
- It states what the company does and why it matters in a way that anyone can summarize without having to quote it literally.
- It avoids jargon, such as "best of breed," "best in class," or vague words such as *superior, expert,* and *empowered.*
- It is affirming, but not grandiose or self-important.
- People easily recognize that it's you.

The statement should be brief because brevity forces you to get to the very heart of what you want to say without larding up your description with empty words or superlatives. Make every word real. Make every word count. Long sentences and vague language can obscure your effort to describe what's really important. At best, they're unhelpful; at worst, they're potentially misleading and distracting.

If you feel your company's strategy is too complex to summarize in one or two paragraphs, that's likely a sign that the strategy itself is unclear, or convoluted in some way.

There is no question that keeping the statement short and to the point is hard work. When an editor once asked Mark Twain for a two-page short story in two days, Twain replied with only mild exaggeration: "No can do 2 pages two days. Can do 30 pages 2 days. Need 30 days to do 2 pages." Even if you aren't very wordy, you'll find that a good brief statement takes revision and polish.

The goal, moreover, is not to write a statement that sounds good: It's to write a statement that *is* good, that really captures your company's distinctiveness. Once you've written and rewritten it, shop it around. Don't show it just to those who work for you or know the business well; give it to acquaintances who don't really know what you do. Ask people to rephrase it in their own words. And don't be surprised if what's mirrored back to you isn't what you intended. That's helpful feedback. Your strategy statement should be able to travel on its own without interpretation and without you there to coach the reader (or the employee, customer, banker, or casual visitor to your website) on what it "really means."

"I know you believe you understood what you think I said but I'm not sure you realise that what you heard was not what I meant..."

Here's the strategy statement constructed by de Mattos for Lance!

To be the prime source of 24-hour-a-day vibrant sports news targeting an audience of passionate, young, male Brazilian sports fans by:
- *Employing 300 sports multi-task journalists to provide exclusive content;*
- *Using the most current technology to deliver content across the widest number of media platforms (print, web, mobile, WebTV and web radio);*

• And using compelling design to enhance all Lance! products;

• All under a powerful core brand, Lance!

• As a means to become one of the most profitable Brazilian media groups as measured by ROI.

And this, in a very different voice, is how Aguiluz constructed the strategy statement for Ink for Less:

Ink for Less aspires to be the largest and most profitable professional ink refilling business by providing

• The best and latest ink refill quality and service

• At reasonable prices

• To our quality conscious but price sensitive individual computer users and small and medium scale business and government institutions

• Through conveniently-located ink refilling stations throughout the major cities and key towns in the Philippines and the rest of Asia.

If you're frustrated with your strategy or with your statement, keep at it. Writing a bad strategy statement is often the necessary prelude to writing a good one. Often what's required is not just wordsmithing—it's "strategy-smithing"—because what you want is a strong, meaningful strategy, not just pretty words. As with many kinds of writing, the words themselves usually aren't the problem; the challenge is the thinking that goes behind them.

HALLMARKS OF GREAT STRATEGIES

Anchored by a clear and compelling purpose
It is said that "if you don't know where you're going, there isn't a road that can get you there." Organizations should exist for a reason. What's yours?

Add real value
Organizations that have a difference that matters add value. If any of them were to go away, they would be missed. Would yours?

Clear choices
Excellence comes from well-defined effort. Attempting to do too many things makes it difficult to do any of them well. What has your business decided to do? To not do?

Tailored system of value creation
The first step in great execution is translating an idea into a system of action, where efforts are aligned and mutually reinforcing. Does this describe your business? In most companies, the true answer is no.

Meaningful metrics
Global outcome measures like ROI indicate whether a strategy is working, but key performance drivers, tailored to your own strategy, are a better indication. They break big aspirations into specific, measurable goals, and guide behavior toward what matters.

Passion
It's a soft concept, but it's at the heart of every great strategy. Even in the most mundane industries, companies that stand out care deeply about what they do.

THE ROAD AHEAD

This exercise should have clarified your thinking and given you an objective, hard look at your business.

If you've been honest with yourself, your thoughtful analysis will likely have brought to the surface problems that should be fixed or areas that require new attention—the bread-and-butter work of a leader-strategist. Some of the problems may be serious: You may need to reconfigure parts of your organization, or find new ways to distinguish yourself. In the worst case, you may have come to the painful realization that you should exit part or all of your business. This can be especially hard when it's close to your heart for one reason or another.

Kerr Taylor had to confront such an issue when he reevaluated his real estate business in the Great Downturn of 2008. Years before, when the company was too big to rely on friends and family but still too small to tap institutional investors, he set up a broker-dealer to help fund real estate purchases. He got the appropriate securities licenses and sold interests to investors, funding the first $25 million of the company's growth. "I couldn't find another way to do it," he says.

Like many companies, AmREIT had to cut back when the economy turned sour. By then Taylor had successfully raised money from the public and through big financial companies, and the broker-dealer no longer offered the company a strategic advantage. Further, the funds needed to operate it could be put to better use. Even so, he was still emotionally attached, "because it was what had brought us along."

The downturn and the experience of clarifying his company's strategy finally pushed him to shut the business down. "It was one of the hardest things I ever did," he says. "That came out of this journey . . . and it's still scary. But it made us grow up."

The process can also strengthen new strategic thrusts, as Miguel Aguiluz discovered. After a number of big businesses asked him for an ink refilling program, he came up with a plan for Ink for Less Professional. Initially he was tempted to simply tack it on to Ink for Less as a "by-the-way" business. But on reflection, he concluded that if he didn't create a whole new system around it, any competitor who came in after him and focused exclusively on business customers would quickly undercut him.

TELLING YOUR STORY: MISTAKES STRATEGISTS MAKE

Carefully honed strategies and the statements that capture them set direction, establish priorities, and guide activity with a firm. They also help you communicate your story externally. Weak strategies and weak statements do the opposite. Avoid these pitfalls.

1. Generic statements
Simply saying you are in book publishing, steel fabrication, or sports marketing tells little. Within that domain, what makes you distinctive? Ask yourself this: If they read your strategy statement, would your customers recognize you? Would your employees? Pixar didn't say it made movies— it said it developed "computer-animated feature films with memorable characters and heartwarming stories that appeal to audiences of all ages."

2. No trade-offs
You can't be everything to everybody, although a lot of weak strategies and strategy statements implicitly claim to be. It doesn't work.

3. Empty clichés
Grand statements unsupported by credible detail are vacuous. Terms such as "Excellent," "Leading," and "Outstanding" don't say anything specific. Strategy statements gain credibility when specific statements capture what a firm does particularly well.

4. Forgetting the means
Many weak statements eagerly tell you the *what* but forget the *how*—the critical activities and resources that enable the firm to realize its competitive advantage. It is through the *how* that a reader gains confidence about what you're doing. Which do you find most convincing: "We're the low-cost producer," or "We're the low-cost producer operating the world's largest titanium dioxide plant utilizing DuPont's proprietary technology"?

5. Leaving out the customer
Who you serve is a crucial part of your story. It not only defines your playing field; it also says who will ultimately decide whether what you do really matters.

6. Deadly dull
There is no other way to say it: A lot of strategy statements in their initial drafts drone on, without conviction, without inspiration. Ask yourself: Would you want to work for this company? Would you want to buy from it?

This insight came to him as he worked his way through an initial strategy wheel for Ink for Less Pro: The activities in the spokes and some of the spokes themselves were markedly different from his consumer business. Employees would have to look more professional, wearing neckties, for instance. He would need to offer new payment terms, to sync with company procurement systems. To provide great service (and create a difference), he determined, each customer should have a "standby refilling technician," to be available when needed. As a result, the products and services would be priced differently. And he wanted to create another market advantage by giving companies printers for free in exchange for a two-year ink contract, not only covering his equipment costs but also keeping competitors at bay. The Pro business is now launched and growing.

This way of thinking has become second nature for Aguiluz. "It's not just for books," he says. "Every time I think of a new business, I really do the strategy wheel," to understand "how I can develop my advantage." As his businesses change or face new competition or other challenges, he goes back to the wheel and examines the whole system, recognizing that a significant change in any part of it is likely to have implications for the rest.

Indeed, when the process works best, a well-defined strategy is like the North Star, guiding you in the right direction no matter which way the competitive winds are blowing. At Lance!, Walter de Mattos has found that strong market share and sizable margins haven't protected the company from competition on all sides. The World Cup is heading to Brazil in 2014, and the country will host the 2016 Olympics, both of which should be a dream opportunity for Lance!—except that the events have spawned new coverage from a number of new players, all competing for the same advertising dollars.

Habits are changing, too. His business was built on quality work produced by a team of specialized journalists. As he watches readers peruse the Internet, de Mattos said, "people are going to seven or eight media outlets in the space of ten minutes," reading so many different short stories that they can't remember what they read or where they read them. "When you see things like that, you have to question your beliefs" about what kinds of information people want, he said. "I have been questioning my beliefs very much lately."

There is "a lot of temptation to change your strategy when something like that happens," he said, but he doesn't think a fundamental change is called for. Instead he is fine-tuning what he calls "gaps" around the wheel in finance, human resources, and technology to strengthen Lance!'s capabilities. The firm remains committed to being the prime source of sports news for Brazil twenty-four hours a day, over all kinds of media platforms.

Your strategy, too, if it is well conceived and on point, will guide you through tumultuous markets, competitive challenges, and your push into new arenas. It will tell you what resources you need to build up and what baggage you should let go. More fundamentally, as you put purpose in the center of your strategic thinking, you will see a shift in the way you look at every opportunity. You will find yourself instinctively asking whether that new business, customer, or product adds value, whether it really fits with what you are doing, and whether it benefits from or enhances the business as a whole. Only then will you truly own your strategy.

Even so, you will continually have to adapt. Shifts in the economy, in your industry, or in your own shop may force you to reconsider your approach and maybe even reinvent it. As we will see in the next chapter, that's why the job of the strategist is never really finished.

7

KEEP IT VIBRANT

WHEN YOUR STRATEGY is on paper, painstakingly crafted, revised, and polished, you'll no doubt feel a huge sense of accomplishment. You'll have a game plan. You'll know where you're going and why. Most managers who go through this rigorous strategy exercise breathe a sigh of relief at the end. My sense is that many of them end up thinking, "I've figured it out. I'm through. The only thing left to do is to put it into gear."

It's not surprising that you or they might think this way. In most popular portrayals the strategist's job would seem to be finished once a carefully articulated strategy has been made ready for implementation. The idea has been formed, the next steps specified, the problem solved. But, as I tell the EOPers, don't get comfortable yet! Rarely can strategy be so neatly contained. There will always be some choices that were not obvious. There will always be countless contingencies, good and bad, that could not have been fully anticipated. There will always be limits to communication and mutual understanding. As Oscar Wilde quipped, "Only the shallow know themselves." At heart, most strategies, like most people, involve some mystery.

Interpreting that mystery is an abiding responsibility of a strategist. Sometimes this entails clarifying a point or helping an organization translate an idea into practice, such as what "best in class" will really mean in that company and how it will be measured. Other times it entails much more: refashioning an element of the strategy, adding a previously missing piece, or reconsidering a commitment that no longer serves the company well.

It is simplistic—dangerous, even—to think that the bulk of strategy work can be done at the beginning and that all a strategist has to do is get that analysis right. Great firms—Nike, Toyota, and Amazon, to name a few—evolve and change. So too do great strategies. No matter how compelling, or how clearly defined, no one strategy is likely to be a sufficient guide for a firm that aspires to a long and prosperous life.

IKEA built a global furniture business not by standing still, but by pushing the design and consumer value envelope for more than fifty years. Gucci rediscovered its brand chic after a fumble that nearly brought the company down. But when I talk to managers about dynamic strategy, I like to delve into the story of Apple, a company that has evolved and reinvented itself more dramatically than perhaps any other over the last three decades.

I have followed Apple over most of those years, and have had countless opportunities to discuss the company's triumphs and follies with groups of executives.[1] The tenor of those discussions has shifted dramatically over the years, with periods of ringing endorsements giving way to years of biting criticism. Either way, the company brings out strong emotions.

There is a lot to learn from Apple's journey, and from the experiences of its remarkable and controversial leader Steve Jobs who, sometimes brilliant and sometimes not, was at the helm long enough (in discontinuous stages) to shape and reshape the company. Beyond the play-by-play, at its core the Apple story challenges us to address some of the most basic truisms of strategy, and, ultimately, to question one of the most foundational: What is the desired result of a strategy?

Academics, venture capitalists, and many managers often say that the goal of strategy is a long-run, sustainable competitive advantage, one that accumulates such a powerful lead over competitors that no one can catch up. In business school cases, analyst reports, and persuasive business plans, the question is repeatedly asked: Is the company there yet? Does it have that killer app, that impermeable edge, that sustainable competitive advantage? But Steve Jobs's story, and the story of Apple itself, cast serious doubts on that aspiration and raise different questions: What does it take for a company to endure? And what does that mean for the work of a strategist?

A RADICAL LEAP FORWARD

Steve Jobs and Steve Wozniak, Apple's cofounders, didn't begin with a statement of purpose. Indeed, in 1977 their ambitions were small as they tried to find customers for Wozniak's all-in-one circuit boards that would eventually be the Apple's heart. Don Valentine, a venture capitalist they met early on, recalls that they imagined selling a couple of thousand boards a year. "They weren't thinking anywhere near big enough," he said.[2]

Not until three years after Apple got off the ground do we find a semblance of a purpose statement, in the 1980 annual report: "Bringing technology to individuals is, we believe, the extraordinary business of this decade." But Wozniak and Jobs didn't want just gee-whiz technology. It had to be special. It had to be unique. It had to be, Jobs would say in time, "insanely great."[3]

I have to remind my classes that the late 1970s were several lifetimes ago in the computer world: IBM did mainframes, and everything else was for hobbyists. The Apple II, launched in 1977 (the company's first real product after a crude prototype) was intended to be a machine that just about any individual could use. It was the first standalone computer that worked right out of the box; with a color display and internal speakers, it could be used for game-playing as well as word processing. Its rounded plastic case, schlocky by today's standards, was a triumph of design compared with hobbyists' crude metal boxes, and was honed by a detail-obsessed Jobs after he studied appliances and stereos at a San Francisco Macy's.[4]

In a significant update the next year, Apple became the first computer company to successfully integrate a floppy disk drive into the computer, replacing the clunky and unreliable cassette drives of the earliest machines.[5] Now users could easily save their own creations and real software could be written and sold. In 1979 that value became crystal clear when Apple added VisiCalc, the first electronic spreadsheet for a personal computer, giving it a clear-cut functional advantage over the Adams, Commodores, Texas Instruments, Radio Shacks, and other newly minted machines.[6]

In this nascent world of personal computers, Apple had a difference that mattered. It staked both its core purpose and its strategic advantage on technology, with the expectation that it was something buyers would always value.

Consumers jumped on board. Apple began to develop a cultlike following among users for its clever design and ease of use. By September 1980, 130,000 Apple IIs had been sold.[7] Wall Street, too, was completely wowed. In 1978 venture capitalists had valued the company at about $3 million. But at the very end of 1980, less than a month after its initial public offering, Apple had a stock market value of $1.8 *billion*. That was more than Chase Manhattan Bank, more than Ford Motor Company, and four times the value of Lockheed Corporation, where Wozniak's father worked.[8]

For all of its technical and design savvy, Apple faced enormous strategic and operational challenges. Wozniak was a genius at building the boxes and Jobs had unstoppable energy and a spot-on sense of style. But neither of them had any management skill or experience. Jobs was known mostly for "causing a lot of waves. He likes to fly around like a hummingbird at ninety miles per hour," one former executive said.[9] He had a reputation for being incredibly difficult—interrupting, failing to listen, missing appointments, and breaking promises.[10] Professional managers were brought in to help manage the growth, but who was calling the shots and who held the power in the organization was not always clear.

Meanwhile the fast-growing industry was changing almost by the day, as one maker after another hurried to bring out new features, more memory, faster processes, better applications, and more useful computers. Eager to maintain its momentum, the Apple team rushed out the Apple III in the summer of 1980 before it had been thoroughly tested—or even really finished. It had little software to offer and was full of bugs, which an attentive technology press was eager to publicize.[11] It was the company's first notable failure.

By then Apple faced its greatest competition yet: The behemoth International Business Machines was now in the business. IBM had taken its time in entering the market, waiting until the pieces were in place for the PC to have genuine business uses. In the rush to catch up, it relied heavily on outsiders, looking to a young Microsoft for an operating system, Intel for the computer's processing brain, and others for memory chips and disk drives. The company's products would never be as elegant or cutting-edge as Apple's but they were hugely practical and they came from a reliable and highly regarded company.

Jobs had a powerful proprietary instinct; he was protective of Apple's still-unique technology and had no interest in opening it up to others. It was a mind-set that would separate the company from most of its competitors—and much of the market—for two decades. IBM, by contrast, made a conscious decision to keep its system open, encouraging software developers to come up with all kinds of word-processing, calculating, accounting, and database software that would make its computers essential to users. The open approach also invited copycat computer makers, but IBM figured (correctly, at least for a time) that its name and reputation would continue to differentiate it.

One meeting around that time is particularly telling: In a 1981 visit with Bill Gates and Paul Allen of Microsoft, Jobs and Gates tangled over where the personal computer was going. Jobs saw the machines as valuable tools for students and homeowners with some uses for business. But Gates was insistent that the PC was a business product first and foremost, a utilitarian business tool, another practical piece of equipment to make the workplace run more efficiently.[12]

These dissimilar approaches would guide the two companies down different roads for many years. With the benefit of hindsight, you and I know where these opposing views will lead. But consider how the landscape looked at that time: Apple was the market share leader in the industry, it had a proprietary state-of-the-art operating system, and a growing base of zealous consumers. Given all of this, and a sky-high stock market price, would you be eager to open your technology to other developers? Would you be convinced, like Bill Gates and IBM, that what the world wanted was a practical business machine that did the job well? Or, like the idealist Jobs, the young leader with a commitment to change the world through technology, would you want to continue on your course to produce your own elegant and cutting-edge products?

INSANELY UNSELLABLE TECHNOLOGY

Sticking to its course, one team at Apple was cleaning up the Apple III while another started on the middle-range Macintosh. Yet another was hard at work on a top-of-the-line revolutionary machine that it named Lisa (presumably after Jobs's daughter). Introduced to great fanfare in 1983, the Lisa was a technological tour de force. PCs then could work on only one program and one screen at a time, and users gave them instructions in a form of code. The Lisa threw all those complexities out the window. It came with the first point-and-click mouse. It had what the techies called a "graphical user interface"—a technical term for menus of options—that could be clicked, making the computer powerful but simple to operate. A user could open more than one function and work on two or three documents at once. The huge leap in possibilities was enough to get an aficionado's heart racing.

As a business proposition, however, the Lisa was a bomb. It cost $50 million and two hundred person-years to develop but it didn't have a clear market. Apple itself had written all the software, none of which was compatible with either the Apple II or IBM machines, and it launched with just a handful of core programs. Further, all the features made the computer painfully slow, while they bloated the price to a heartburn-inducing $10,000.[13]

It would be hard to change the world with stunning technology that no one bought. Lisa "was a great machine. We just couldn't sell any," said Bruce Tognazzini, Apple's human interface guru.[14]

Jobs himself had been so combative and disruptive during the development of the Lisa that he was removed from it midstream and banished to the Macintosh project, which was being developed in an isolated location that would separate him from the rest of the company. Despite the disappointment, he "set off with guns blazing to make the Macintosh the world's next groundbreaking computer."[15]

Before it could be rolled out, however, he had to contend with another management challenge: finding a replacement for Apple's president, who had resigned following the disappointing sales of the Apple III and the round of downsizing that followed. Jobs, who became chairman during the reshuffling at the top, personally recruited John Sculley, president of PepsiCo, who had helped drive Pepsi briefly past Coke as the nation's top soft drink. Jobs wooed him for many months, reportedly winning Sculley when he asked, "Do you want to spend the rest of your life selling sugared water, or do you want a chance to change the world?"[16] In Job's mind, Apple's purpose was clear.

Sculley arrived in time to help launch the Macintosh in 1984. It debuted to huge fanfare, propelled by a famous Super Bowl ad, pegged to the Orwellian year, that characterized the new computer as rescuing users from a drone-like existence. While IBM and its copycats were still using clunky DOS-prompt commands, the Mac offered elegant and simply designed graphics, a mouse, and far more flexibility.

But the Macintosh needed work. The reviews—and sales—were

decidedly tepid. At a premium price of $2,495, it was slow, incompatible with the developing MS-DOS standards, and lacking a range of software at a time when programs for IBM machines were making them more and more useful. For the first time in its history, Apple was in serious trouble. Its competitive advantage—and its poignant purpose—were slipping away. It soon reported its first quarterly loss and plans to lay off one-fifth of its workforce.

Jobs, the high-energy visionary, was not getting the job done. Moreover, he and Sculley by then were at irreconcilable odds over Apple's strategy. In Jobs's mind, "Apple was supposed to become a wonderful consumer products company," Sculley wrote in his memoir. But the business market, not the consumer market, was exploding in the mid-1980s and Sculley thought pursuing the consumer business in that context was "a lunatic plan."[17]

Jobs, the thirty-year-old wunderkind, who had been on the cover of *BusinessWeek*, *Time*, and a host of other magazines, who had brought cutting-edge products to a host of users, had failed as company leader. True, his Apple was creative and innovative, but it was increasingly out of sync with the industry, which was aiming not at consumers but at cost-conscious businesses in need of more productivity.

With the support of the board, Sculley stripped Jobs of all his operational responsibilities. It was a huge blow to the charismatic big thinker who was the public face of Apple Computer. "I feel like somebody punched me in the stomach and knocked all my wind out," Jobs told an interviewer. "I know I've got at least one more great computer in me. And Apple is not going to give me a chance to do that."[18]

Before the end of the year, Jobs would leave Apple and form a new computer maker, NeXT.

THE SUPER-MANAGER ERA

When a company founder flails, an outside manager often steps in. But would a super-manager read the market better? Could professional executives do a better job restoring Apple's onetime competitive edge—or restore or generate a more meaningful purpose?

Under Sculley, Apple became a more disciplined, if less creative, company. The Mac's problems were cleaned up, winning intensely devoted fans. Capitalizing on its strengths, including an advanced printer, Sculley helped the company become the leader in the burgeoning field of desktop publishing, allowing legions of users to create their own fliers, pamphlets, and professional-looking documents for the first time.

But while Apple had inroads in schools and with graphic artists, IBM computers and their clones became the de facto machines for the workplace. They weren't pretty, they weren't all that easy to use, and they certainly weren't fun. But thanks to a storm of software, they could build intricate spreadsheets, create complex documents with ease, capture large amounts of data, and—significantly—easily share it with any other similar computer. Networks of these relatively powerful computers already were changing office productivity like nothing seen since the mainframes of the 1960s.

Under Sculley's watch, more than 12 million Macs were sold as the market for personal computers began to boom, and the company's sales grew to almost $8 billion from a mere $600 million when Sculley joined the firm in 1983.[19] But Apple's market share, which had peaked in mid-1984 at 21.82 percent, was sliding.[20] The once-innovative company struggled vainly to introduce trendsetting products. Its first portable machine—the hot computer product of the 1990s—was too big, too heavy, and late to the party. A pre-Palm, pre-BlackBerry personal digital assistant (PDA) called Newton had the potential to be groundbreaking but turned out to be ahead of its time. With deteriorating margins, no answers to increasing price competition, and few successful new products, Sculley himself was pushed out in 1993.[21]

His successor, Michael Spindler, was a no-nonsense manager who had tripled the size of Apple's European business. Spindler set out to cut costs, declaring that Apple's products would never be overpriced again. He reduced R&D spending, improved efficiency, and cut development cycles. He also broke with the company's long-standing proprietary philosophy and tried to license Apple's technology, but pulled back after clones cannibalized the company's sales.

Without a viable purpose and a well-aligned system, Spindler, like Sculley, failed to stem the tide of buyers who were rapidly defecting to computers powered by Intel processors and running Windows operating systems. A 1995 *Computer World* survey of 140 corporate computer system managers found that none of the Windows users would consider buying a Mac, while more than half the Apple users expected to buy an Intel-based PC.[22] In apparent desperation, Spindler tried to sell the company. But other computer makers, struggling themselves with declining margins and wicked global competition, couldn't see much future in what Apple had to offer.

Spindler was out in three years, replaced in 1996 by company director Gil Amelio, whose tenure would be even shorter. When Amelio took over, Apple was leaking cash and sales were plunging. The Apple operating system was in need of a major overhaul. The brand, which had mattered so much to customers in its early days, was now less and less significant. Microsoft had copied many of its best features and the differences between how IBM and Apple computers worked had narrowed.

Shortly after he took charge, Amelio shared his perspective on the company's challenges at a Silicon Valley cocktail party: "Apple is a boat," he told listeners, according to a guest who was there. "There's a hole in the boat, and it's taking on water. But there's also a treasure on board. And the problem is, everyone on board is rowing in different directions, so that boat is just standing still. My job is to get everyone rowing in the same direction so we can save the treasure."

After Amelio turned away, the guest turned to the person next to him with an obvious question: "But what about the hole?"[23]

Indeed, what about the hole?

Amelio tried to patch it with the skills he'd honed in turning around semiconductor businesses at Rockwell International and National Semiconductor. He shrank the product line, slashed payrolls, and rebuilt cash reserves. His strategy, he said, would be to return Apple to its historical premium-priced game by aiming at higher-margin segments, such as servers, Internet access devices, and PDAs.

But no matter how hard Apple rowed, it didn't work. The company's quality had become questionable, and its nearly ten-year-old operating system was under assault by a worthy competitor, Windows 95. Amelio decided to cut Apple's losses by canceling the repeatedly delayed next-generation Mac OS, which had already cost more than $500 million in R&D. To replace it, he turned to none other than Steve Jobs for a version of his NeXTStep software, designed for high-end personal computers and servers. Paying what many thought was an absurd price, Apple bought NeXT in 1997 for $400 million, bringing Jobs back into the fold as an advisor. But as Apple's downhill slide continued, Amelio himself came under fire. By the end of the first quarter of 1997, the company had lost $1.6 billion during his tenure. The board sent him packing with a nice golden parachute and named Jobs interim CEO.[24]

THE ROTTING CORE

What can strategists learn from Apple's experience? The fundamental lesson is the evanescence of a difference that matters. It doesn't last by itself, and when it's gone, no amount of rowing or patching of the hull can fix the basic problem: The ship has lost its rudder.

The Austrian-American economist Joseph Schumpeter, writing in the 1940s, saw developments like this as part of an economic cycle. Innovators break new ground and reap what he called "economic rents," outsized profits for their innovative endeavors. The most potent of these developments cause, in his words, "creative destruction," world-shaking innovations that reorder a marketplace. These foment a "competition which commands a decisive cost or quality advantage which strikes not at the margins of the profits and the outputs of the existing firms but at their foundations and their very lives."[25]

Such creative destruction comes with its own cycle. First the idea evolves, followed by its commercialization—much like the Apple II moved computers from the hobbyists' garages into people's homes. In time, other competitors see the abundant opportunities and find their way in, pushing up output and driving down prices, until the economic rents have all but disappeared. Another round of creative destruction must take place for profits to leap forward again. This was exactly the kind of erosion Apple sought to avoid as it rushed the Apple III, Lisa, and Macintosh computers to market.

The creative destruction that beset Apple, though, was not the kind of product innovation at which the company itself excelled, but a market innovation: the benefits that IBM's commitment to open sourcing, and the ensuing standardization, brought to business users and software developers. In its initial phases, the strategy produced high growth and profits for IBM, but in a span of less than twenty years, it drove the industry from an attractive, profitable business to a viciously competitive, price-driven one. Thanks to their compatibility and simple off-the-shelf components, PCs largely became a commodity and sales shifted to the most efficient and cheapest providers. Among PC manufacturers themselves, there was little asymmetry to be found. By 2001, 96.5 percent of profit in the industry was captured by two suppliers who controlled the only scarce resources: Microsoft, with its industry standard MS-DOS operating system, and Intel, with branded processors that were the brains of the machines. Dell's star also rose during this period, not because it made particularly outstanding computers, but because it mastered mass customization, electronic commerce, and supply-chain management.[26]

Many of the longtime players would disappear over the next decade or so. Compaq and Gateway were acquired and IBM sold its PC business in 2004, after losing nearly $1 billion since the turn of the century.[27] In this milieu, Apple was slain, in part, by the same dragon that got Manoogian at Masco: tenacious and unattractive industry forces. Like Manoogian, many of Apple's leaders didn't fully appreciate or respect the dramatic impact that deteriorating industry forces would have on Apple's prospects.

They were, to put it bluntly, arrogant. An observer of the early days commented: "Everybody at Apple sits around and says, 'We're the best. We know it.' They have a culture that says it and it starts from Steve Jobs and works on down."[28] Another noted that the "arrogance seeped right through the company and came to affect every aspect of the business— the style with which it treated suppliers, software firms, and dealers, its attitudes toward competitors, and the way it approached the development of new products."[29]

When a firm's purpose is consistent with the competitive environment and produces a difference that matters, it's compelling. When it grows out of sync and anchors a firm in a past that no longer exists, it's a liability. Apple was essentially caught in a trap of its own making, out of sync with a computer market that had become increasingly connected and commoditized. It stubbornly stuck to its original strategy of producing expensive and clever personal computers that used different processors and required different software (and even printers) than everyone else. The super-managers who carried on after Jobs scrambled to fix problems with layoffs, restructurings, and flip-flopping strategies about whether to move to an open system, reduce prices, or enter segments with higher margins, but most didn't grapple deeply enough with the fundamental question you know so well:

Is the very core, the purpose behind it all, working?

Looking back, Apple cofounder Steve Wozniak rued the firm's refusal to test its core assumptions, particularly the decision to keep a tight hold on the operating system to protect what executives thought was Apple's critical resource—its hardware. In fact, in the competitive milieu that developed, it was Apple's software, not hardware, that would have been the most valuable to users.

"We had the most beautiful operating system, but to get it you had to buy our hardware at twice the price. That was a mistake," Wozniak said. "What we should have done was calculate an appropriate price to license the operating system."[30] While the early builders thought that better technology would always prevail, they learned the hard way that it was just one dimension the market cared about, and not enough to overcome the disadvantages of the full package.

"The computer was never the problem," Wozniak said. "The company's strategy was."[31]

THE EDUCATION OF A STRATEGIST

The Jobs who left Apple in 1985 was a cocky and brash young manager, determined to demonstrate that he could win with the Apple strategy of making cutting edge computers with great technology. At NeXT, Jobs was in complete control—and by all accounts, he ran rampant, unchecked by the kinds of professional managers who tempered his energy at Apple or even a board of directors. His almost impossibly high standards ruled, as Alan Deutschman described: "It wasn't enough for the new machine to be distinguished by one particular breakthrough. For the software he was taking an entirely new approach, starting from scratch, trying to create the most elegant lines of software code ever written. The industrial design had to be like no computer ever created. It had to be as gorgeous and sleek as Steve's black Porsche. Even the *factory* had to be beautiful, and it had to be as fully automated as any factory in the world."[32]

NeXT's first computer, a gorgeous cube design Jobs described as "five years ahead of its time," was aimed at the academic market. But it was late arriving and—at $10,000 if you bought a laser printer and some necessary extras—priced closer to a Volkswagen than a PC. Commercially, the machine was a colossal failure, a caricature writ large of Apple's failed strategy, and the responsibility lay fully at Jobs's own feet. Students and academics shunned the cube for $1,500 basic PCs. The business world wasn't much interested, either. While too expensive to be a personal computer, the computer was too underpowered to be a workstation.[33] As he had at Apple, Jobs again misread the market and what it wanted. Ultimately, NeXT sold just 50,000 machines, a pitiful result.[34]

Jobs's star fell dramatically in Silicon Valley as his chance to show that he could "do it" again faded. It was an embarrassing personal debacle. As early as 1993, top managers had begun to rush for the exits, the contents of the factory were being auctioned off, and *Fortune* magazine had dubbed Jobs a "snake-oil salesman."[35] Reflecting later on the fiasco, Jobs explained: "We knew we'd either be the last hardware company that made it or the first that didn't, and we were the first that didn't."[36]

During the same period, however, Jobs was involved in another venture that would prove more durable. After leaving Apple, he sold nearly all his stock, and used some of the proceeds to buy a majority interest in Pixar, a fledgling animation studio. Though he was more of a venture capitalist there than an executive, he held the title of chairman and CEO, and bankrolled the company through a number of downturns. As *Toy Story*, the first feature-length computer-generated film, was about to be released in 1995, Jobs stepped up his involvement and orchestrated Pixar's enormously successful initial public offering (which netted him $1.17 billion). Following the IPO, he negotiated a new five-film deal with Disney, which produced *Toy Story 2*, *Monsters Inc.*, and *Finding Nemo*, films that broke all conventions in animated storytelling. In 2006, when Disney bought Pixar for $7.5 billion, Jobs became a Disney director and the entertainment firm's largest shareholder.[37] For Jobs, Pixar turned out to have a Disney-like ending: It made him a multibillionaire, helped him rebuild his reputation in the business community, and gave him contacts and deep insights into the entertainment industry, which would become important later.

REDISCOVERING DIFFERENCES THAT MATTER

NeXT was barely hanging on when Apple bought it, and the industry had all but written Apple itself off. When Jobs returned, the company was rapidly slipping toward bankruptcy. Its stock price was at a ten-year low and its market share had plummeted to 3 percent. Speaking at an industry conference, Michael Dell, the chairman and CEO of Dell Computer, had a sharp answer for what he would do if he woke up suddenly in the form of Steve Jobs: "I'd shut Apple down and give the money back to shareholders."[38]

But Jobs, educated by his NeXT and Pixar experiences, stepped up to the challenge. He began the painstaking process of rebuilding his old company, following advice he himself had given the year before: "If I were running Apple, I would milk the Macintosh for all it's worth—and get busy on the next great thing," he told *Fortune* in 1996.[39]

Jobs began by cutting Apple's broad product line to four offerings— two consumer, two business, a portable and a desktop model each—and targeting research and development on the very best ideas. Of these, the first product conceived and built after Jobs's return was the iMac. "The day I left Apple we had a 10-year lead over Microsoft. In the technology business a 10-year lead is really hard to come by . . . [but], if you look at the Mac that ships today, it's 25 percent different than the day I left. And that's not enough for 10 years and billions of dollars in R&D," he said, looking back. "It wasn't that Microsoft was so brilliant or clever in copying the Mac, it's that the Mac was a sitting duck for 10 years.

"That's Apple's problem: their differentiation evaporated."[40]

By the following year, Jobs had put a new management team in place, including several managers who had worked with him at NeXT. This team would be the core of his brain trust for nearly ten years.[41] The new Jobs also had a new management style. By all accounts, he was still brash, abrasive, and often arrogant, but this Jobs knew something about executing and had enough maturity to temper his worst behaviors. During the first meeting with a product group, Steve reportedly would "listen and absorb. In the second meeting, he would ask a series of difficult and provocative questions: 'If you had to cut half of your products, what would you do?' he would ask. He would also take a positive tack: 'If money were no object, what would you do?'"[42]

The iMac, introduced in 1998, was a well-designed all-in-one computer and monitor, with a price tag of $1,299—still higher than popular

PCs, but well below the $2,000-plus of previous models. Its design was a breath of fresh air in a market that had seen little fundamental innovation in some time, incorporating the simplicity of the original Mac and an easy way to use the Internet. It quickly attracted a whole new customer group—nearly 30 percent of those who bought an iMac had never owned a computer before. In the first year, Apple sold two million of the machines, which, with cost cutting, helped it build a much-needed cash cushion.[43]

In effect, with the iMac, Jobs patched the hole in Apple's boat.

Jobs put the cash to work with a new strategy, one that combined the firm's original purpose with an incisive understanding of what consumers valued. At a MacWorld gathering in 2001, he spelled out a greater purpose for Apple. The first golden age of the personal computer, the age of productivity, he explained, began with the early machines and lasted about fifteen years. That was followed by a second golden age, the age of the Internet, which brought new uses to both businesses and consumers.

Now, he said, the computer was entering a third great age, the digital age, populated by cell phones, DVD players, digital cameras, and digital music. In that new age, Jobs thought, the "next great thing" would be the computer not as another gadget, but as the centerpiece of all these devices. It would pull together information management, communication, and entertainment in a seamless whole, enhancing how all these other devices could be used. Now you would be able to both take video and edit it, listen to music and create your own mixes and sounds, record your pictures and share them in new and different ways.[44]

This so-called digital hub strategy became a new purpose, a clear, well-articulated idea that would guide Apple's products and strategy for the next decade. As it began to take shape, Apple introduced the iTunes music software as a way to organize music on your computer, rolled out a fully overhauled Mac operating system, and opened its first retail store, selling Apple products in high-tech, high-touch boutiques, complete with customer-service "genius bars."

Piece by piece, Jobs began to remake Apple. It was not always a smooth or linear process. Perhaps drawing from his Pixar experience, Jobs initially pushed iMovie, software that would allow Mac users to easily make and edit movies. But while he focused on that, users were gorging themselves on services that were providing digital music for free and using burners installed on many PCs to make their own compact discs. The iMac hadn't yet offered CD burners, and without them, sales slowed.

Jobs had a forehead-slapping moment. "I felt like a dope," he said. "I thought we had missed it. We had to work hard to catch up."[45]

An upgrade to the Mac Operating System addressed the problem, then Apple designers saw another opportunity: The available digital music players were awful. They were slow to load and they could hold only a few songs—an improvement over the Sony Walkman, to be sure, but hardly products for a digital age. The iPod, introduced in late 2001, was a sea change, a powerful music player that would fit easily in a pocket thanks to a tiny hard drive and an Apple software called FireWire that allowed for superfast downloading.

With it and iTunes, Apple revolutionized the music industry. Napster, a popular file-sharing software, had conditioned users to the idea of downloading their own music choices for free, a service that was later declared illegal. Jobs struck a deal with the music industry: Apple would provide a similar service with iTunes but charge for individual songs and albums, and the industry would share in the revenues. The iTunes store opened for Mac users in April 2003 and expanded to Windows users that October, multiplying its market exponentially. (In another sign of a new age, Apple developed software explicitly to make something work as elegantly on a PC as it did on the iMac.) And in a rare economic turnaround, consumers began to pay for something that had recently been free.

The products and services Apple rolled out capitalized on the company's exquisite sense of design and technological wizardry and brought the whole digital revolution into sharp relief. Jobs told *Time* in early 2002, "I would rather compete with Sony than compete in another product category with Microsoft."[46]

There's another boat story, an ancient Greek paradox that provides a powerful metaphor for this process. After slaying the Minotaur in Crete, the hero Theseus sailed back to Athens in a well-worn ship. As each plank decayed, it was replaced by new and stronger timber, until every plank in the ship had been changed. Was it then still the same ship? And if not, then at what point—with which plank—did the ship's identity shift? It's a paradox that Plutarch called "the logical question of things that grow."[47]

At Apple, Jobs saw the iPod as a turning point. "If there was ever a product that catalyzed what's Apple's reason for being, it's this," he said, "because it combines Apple's incredible technology base with Apple's legendary ease of use with Apple's awesome design. Those three things come together in this, and it's like, *that's what we do.* So if anybody was ever wondering why is Apple on earth, I would hold up this as a good example."[48]

By 2005, a total of 42 million iPods had been sold.[49] By 2009, Apple was selling 60 million *a year.* Users downloaded more than a billion songs off iTunes and now bought movies, television shows, and even business school lectures for their iPods.

If the iMac had helped Jobs stabilize the boat, the iPod and iTunes were now propelling the whole enterprise forward as a new vessel with a new purpose and a new destination. And, as with Gucci, it was becoming clear that Apple's success was due not to a host of one-off products, but from honing an idea, an identity, and an intricately woven system of elements that worked in concert.

Intuitively, Jobs understood Schumpeter's message about "creative destruction," and this time got ahead of the curve. The new Apple, under the new Jobs, became its own "creative destruction" machine, leaning into the wind to introduce better and better products that cannibalized themselves, seemingly before anyone else had a chance to get within half a mile.

In 2007, Apple rolled out the iPhone, leveraging the special design of the iPod into a credit card–sized package that could take and make calls, talk to the Internet, and hold vast amounts of music or photos as well. Suddenly a good bit of the equipment on your desk fit easily into your pocket, and the company was en route to revolutionizing another industry.

Fittingly, that year, Apple dropped "Computer" from its name and became simply Apple Inc. By 2010, computers made up just 27 percent of its $65.2 billion in sales for the fiscal year ended September 25, while iPods, music, and iPhones brought in almost 60 percent of the revenue.[50] Apple's stock roared to unseen heights. With a market value well over $300 billion, it became the most valuable technology company in the world, surpassing Microsoft.

Even as Jobs battled serious health problems, including a 2009 liver transplant, Apple trumped itself again, introducing the much-anticipated tablet computer, the iPad. The design, the capabilities, and the software set new standards for a whole new category of portable consumer devices, which may, in the not-too-distant future, replace the traditional computer altogether. The beta version of the much-touted iCloud, announced in the summer of 2011, was a further step, allowing users to keep data in sync between any Apple or PC with no need to transfer files by email or USB.[51]

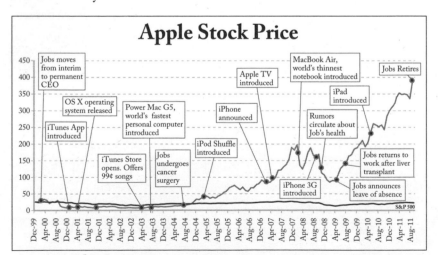

A SUSTAINABLE COMPETITIVE ADVANTAGE?

Given this grand transformation, it's appropriate to ask: Is Apple there yet? Despite its late-century troubles, does it now have a sustainable competitive advantage?

I often ask EOPers this question when teaching the Apple case. It is tempting to shout, *"Yes!,"* as classes often do, or maybe even retort, "Do you have to ask?" Apple has reinvented its innovative purpose and, on the face of it, seems to be running circles around competitors, even taunting them for their lack of creativity. Case closed?

I think not.

In 2010, Apple's computer market share soared to about 11 percent, but that's hardly the mark of a dominant industry player. Otherwise normal people will camp outside an Apple store for the latest iPhone, but smartphones based on Google Inc.'s Android software substantially outsold the iPhone in 2010, according to NPD Group, a market research firm.[52] Windows-based competitors to the iPad are coming fast and furiously. Such tablets might well become the fourth golden age, replacing the traditional personal computer as the center of the digital hub while becoming products sold largely on price. And there's no guarantee that the iPad, the iCloud ecosystem, or their successors will be the ones that head the pack a couple of years from now.

Conventional wisdom would say that the goal of strategy is a long-term sustainable competitive advantage. I challenge that view. Such advantages are rare and for good reason. As Schumpeter showed, peaks in market growth and profitability often come from change, not stasis. Henry Ford dominated car sales with a single, affordable model until Alfred Sloan's General Motors beat him with a line of differentiated products. Polaroid owned instant photography until digital imaging shut it out; many broad-service hospitals were monopolies until low-cost focused providers started chipping away at their base; colleges with sprawling campuses owned higher education until community colleges, for-profit organizations, and distance learning challenged them with different economic models.

Zeroing in on one competitive advantage and expecting it to be sustainable misrepresents the strategist's challenge. It encourages managers to see their strategies as set in concrete and, when spotting trouble ahead, to go into defensive mode, hunkering down to protect the status quo instead of rising to meet the needs of a new reality. To be sure, competitive advantage is essential to strategy, and the longer it lasts, the better. But any one advantage, even a company's underlying system of value creation, is only part of a bigger story, one frame in a motion picture. It is the need to manage *across* frames, day by day, year over year, that makes a leader's role in strategy so vital.

This organic view of strategy recognizes that whatever constitutes strategic advantage will eventually change. It underscores the difference between defending a firm's added value as established at any given moment and something far more important: ensuring that a firm continues to add value over time. *This* is what endures—not a particular purpose, a particular advantage, or a particular strategy, but the ongoing need to add value, always. The ongoing need to guide and develop a company so that it continues to matter. This is not to say that great resources and great advantages are not built by businesses that enhance their core differences over time. But the products and services that embody those differences must evolve and change and, as Apple learned the hard way, their value has to be measured by the present environment, not one that once was.

Quite painfully, that may mean that, like the ship of Theseus, the keel may need to be rebuilt or the ship may need to sail in a very different direction. As my executive students like to point out, this challenge rarely happens when you're sitting at the dock. It's a hard realization that the planks have to be changed while you're sailing, while you're also straining to navigate and working hard to keep the ship afloat.

On his return to Apple, Jobs had to remake the computer company plank by plank while also keeping it from bankruptcy—rebuilding not in a rainstorm, but in a hurricane on the high seas. He got it right for the

most part, but, as even its archrival—the once undauntable Microsoft—
has discovered, the challenge never ends.

ON BEING A STRATEGIST—EVEN WHEN YOU'RE NOT STEVE JOBS

"Okay," you may be thinking about now, "I get that strategy must
be dynamic. I accept that by most measures, Apple is a strategic success.
And Steve Jobs really turned it around. But let's be fair: He was Steve
Jobs—and I'm not. Nor is my company Apple." It's a reaction I often
hear from executives.

You're right, of course. There was only one Jobs. But among the
remarkable chapters of his story is that he wasn't a born strategist. He
made huge mistakes. He introduced flawed products. He drove one
company into the ground, and was himself driven from another. He had
to learn to be a strategist, just like the rest of us.

Like De Sole at Gucci, Jobs had to have the energy and motivation to keep an enterprise moving forward. He had to wrestle with the
profound and terrible paradox many strategists must manage: Stay the
course—Reinvent yourself. This may sound like a choice between con-
tinuing on a given path or choosing another, but for most businesses it's
usually a duality: being one thing while becoming something else. This
points to another advantage for a firm: the strategist—or, more specifically, you. As a strategist, you're the person who must watch over the
organization, guiding its course, making the choices that bring it back
to center day after day and year after year even as you must choose when
the center, the purpose, itself should evolve. You must decide whether
to lean into the wind or not, and judge whether your strategy is dynamic
or dead.

Leading strategy is a nonstop responsibility; it can't be outsourced
or solved in one great brainstorming session. You won't just wake up one
day to find that your company has a new advantage or that its purpose
changed overnight. Rather, it will change because the industry changes.

It will change because tastes change. It will change because your people change and they bring new skills and strengths to the enterprise. And ultimately, it will change because someone made the call to do so—you, the strategist.

Now, having accepted that the only sustainable strategy is one that anticipates change, you're ready to embrace becoming the strategist who takes your company where it needs to go.

8

THE ESSENTIAL STRATEGIST

WE'VE TALKED A great deal about what a strategist does, but we've touched only lightly on the *person* who does it. For all the information available on strategy, little is devoted to what will make you a successful strategist. What skills and mind-sets do you need to hone? What unique value could you bring to your business?

My final task is to address these questions, and to help you be the strategist you want to be. Unlike so much of the work you've done up to here, this last leap requires putting aside the industry analyses and the strategy statements, and instead looking deeply into the *how* of being a strategist.

The most important thing is to understand that you are not a manager of strategy, or a functional specialist. Others can fill those roles. You are, first and foremost, a leader. Your goal is to build something that is not already there. To do so, you must confront the four basic questions you have already explored:

What does my organization bring to the world?
Does that difference matter?
Is something about it scarce and difficult to imitate?

Are we doing today what we need to do in order to matter tomorrow?

As a leader, you must answer these questions.

Most business practitioners (and most business thinkers, for that matter) are unaccustomed to facing questions of this kind—at least when put so starkly. We're much more comfortable confining ourselves to more tangible business issues: Is our market shrinking or growing? What are our competitors up to? To lead, you have to be willing to make room for new challenges and be open to the unique ways you can add value to your business. Think about this old Zen story. A powerful and self-assured man goes to a Zen master and asks to be taught about enlightenment. After sizing up the guest in an initial conversation, the Zen master invites him to have tea. The master pours. He goes on pouring even though the tea is flowing over the brim of the cup.

"Stop!" the visitor calls out. "Can't you see that the cup is overflowing?"

"Yes," the Zen master replies. "But a cup that is already full cannot take in anything else." If one's mind is already filled to the brim, there is no place for new ideas.

To be a strategist, one must be willing to explore new ways of leading.

BE A FIRE STARTER

Being a strategist takes drive and initiative, and the willingness and curiosity to ask questions and venture forward. As bedrock important as strategy is to the long-term success of a firm, you might think that investors, boards of advisors, even those working in a firm would keep it uppermost in a leader's mind. Unfortunately, the opposite is too often true; parties you'd think would be clamoring for more settle for less, especially if a business's numbers are reasonably good. The commitment and passion—the fire starting—for this work must come from you.

But leaders themselves, and their own schedules, are often part of the problem.

Finding the time and courage to address strategy is a constant challenge for most leaders. Sure, you know you need to work on strategy now and then, and you recognize that your management team needs it. But you're the one who has to make space for it and that rarely is easy. "Managers who get caught in the trap of overwhelming demands become prisoners of routines," wrote Heike Bruch and Sumantra Ghoshal, in *A Bias for Action*. "They do not have time to notice opportunities. Their habituated work prevents them from taking the first necessary step toward harnessing willpower: developing the capacity to dream an idea into existence and transforming it into a concrete intention."[1]

Stephen Covey's celebrated distinction between urgent and important activities helps us understand, in part, why this is so. Too often people are consumed by activities that are urgent but not important—interruptions, many day-to-day activities, and common fires every manager faces. What suffers are endeavors that are important but not urgent: building organizational capabilities, nurturing long-term relationships, and developing viable strategies.

Beyond competing demands and the adrenaline rush that comes with constant activity, there is an even deeper explanation about why many leaders, and many firms, fail to fully engage with strategy: They're comfortable with the status quo even when it isn't scintillating. Schumpeter warned long ago that most people are content with keeping things the way they are. Richard Swedberg, a Schumpeter expert, notes that the conservative nature of people pushes back against innovation, and many leaders themselves resist change: "While doing what is familiar is always easy . . . doing what is new is not."[3] Or, as Schumpeter said, "The whole difference between swimming with the stream and against the stream is to be found here."[4]

For economic development to flourish, leaders must swim against the stream. They must step forward and take the initiative, energetically showing the way. Schumpeter refers to this type of leader as a "Man of Action" (Mann der Tat), someone who does not accept reality as it is.

The Man of Action, in Swedberg's interpretation, "does not have the same inner obstacles to change as static people or people who avoid doing what is new. What then drives the man of action? In contrast the static person, who goes about his business because he wants to satisfy his needs and stops once his goal has been accomplished, the leader has other sources of motivation. He charges ahead because he wants power and because he wants to accomplish things . . ."[5]

Behind every pulsating, vibrant successful strategy is a leader who seized the initiative and made it happen. Developing and executing strategy with all the necessary dimensions—including the accountability that attends to making decisions with great consequences—is not a function. It is a leadership job, and a big one.

IT'S YOUR CHOICE

In a now classic *Harvard Business Review* article, published in 1963, the year before the first women were admitted to the MBA program, Seymour Tilles, a lecturer at the school, wrote about the responsibility leaders have for setting a course for a company. He proposed that of all the questions a chief executive is required to answer, one predominates: What kind of company do you want yours to be? (He raised a similar question for aspiring leaders about themselves.) Wrote Tilles:

> *If you ask young men what they want to accomplish by the time they are 40, the answers you get fall into two distinct categories. There are those—the great majority—who will respond in terms of what they want to have. This is especially true of graduate students of business administration. There are some men, however, who will answer in terms of the kind of men they hope to be. These are the only ones who have a clear idea of where they are going.*
> *The same is true of companies. For far too many companies, what little thinking goes on about the future is done primarily in*

*money terms. There is nothing wrong with financial planning.
Most companies should do more of it. But there is a basic fallacy in
confusing a financial plan with thinking about the kind of company
you want yours to become. It is like saying, "When I'm 40, I'm
going to be rich." It leaves too many basic questions unanswered.
Rich in what way? Rich doing what?*[6]

In the last three decades, as strategy has moved to become a science, we have allowed this fundamental insight to slip away. We need to bring it back. Existentialist philosophers understood the importance of choices. They recognized that as individuals, who we are is to a large extent an accumulation of all the choices, large and small, we've made through the years of our lives. External events and influences are important, too, but our choices are the most powerful lever we have to affect our lives.

So, too, for companies. But who makes the vital choices that determine a firm's very identity? Who says, "*This* is our purpose, not that. *This* is who we will be. *This* is why our customers and clients will prefer a world with us rather than without us"? These are the questions the strategist must own. While existence may be given, essence never is. The story, the meaning, the real significance must be made. As a leader, it is yours to create. Others, inside and outside the firm, will contribute in meaningful ways, but in the end, it is the leader who bears responsibility for the choices that are made.

It is this responsibility that gives you a profound opportunity to shape your business and influence its destiny. Or as Jean-Paul Sartre, a major exponent of existentialism, put it, "There is a future to be fashioned."[7] Sartre championed what he called "the possibility of choice," celebrating the way it positions people to craft identity and define purpose. In his view, it is this fundamental aspect—the possibility of choice—that creates the opportunity to find meaning. "Man first of all exists," he writes, "encounters himself, surges up in the world—and defines himself afterwards."[8] Sartre's is a universe that creates boundless possibilities for self-definition.

Now consider the meaning this conviction, this faith in the power of individuals to "surge up in the world," "invent themselves," and "fashion a future" can hold in the business world. Isn't this what Schumpeter was saying? Isn't it what business should be all about? Managers trying to sustain strategic perspective must be ready to confront this basic challenge. Organizations have to "surge up," "invent themselves," and "fashion" their futures. They too face what Sartre calls a "possibility of choice" every day their doors are open. Or rather, their owners and managers do, for just as Sartre assigns people responsibility for fashioning their futures, the strategic imperative for organizations falls to those who lead them.

This quest is as relevant for large multibusiness companies as it is for focused, owner-led ones. As leveraged buy-outs proliferate and supply chains open up around the world, nothing is more important for any firm than a clear sense of purpose, a clear sense of why they matter. A board chairman at one such conglomerate made the point bluntly when he asked, "What hot dish is this company bringing to the table?" He was issuing the same challenge.

Such work can take enormous courage and fortitude—the way Young and Kohl at Brighton Collectibles insist on minimum resale prices and refuse to sell to stores that won't provide sufficient marketing support for their brand, or the way Ingvar Kamprad chose to produce furniture for the many, not the few. These are the decisions that determine not only what a business will do, but, more fundamentally, what a business will be. Few choices could matter more.

STAY AGILE

As we saw with Apple, the strategist's work is never done. Achieving and maintaining strategic momentum is a challenge that confronts an organization and its leader every day of their entwined existence. It's not one choice a strategist must make, but multiple choices over time.

Helmuth von Moltke, a disciple of the military theorist Clausewitz, understood this well: "Certainly the commander in chief will keep his great objective continuously in mind, undisturbed by the vicissitudes of events. But the path on which he hopes to reach it can never be firmly established in advance. Through the campaign he must make a series of decisions on the basis of situations that cannot be foreseen. . . . Everything depends on penetrating the uncertainty of veiled situations to evaluate facts, to clarify the unknown, to make decisions rapidly, and then to carry them out with strength and constancy."[9]

No less than for the military commander, this is your job, and it's a challenging balancing act. As we learned in previous chapters, great strategies are systems, with their own integrity and internal harmony among the elements (think of how De Sole rigorously linked everything he did to his purpose, from product line on up to management culture). Often, you will be able to adapt while keeping your purpose intact. But you cannot confuse the integrity of a system with rigidity. Your system of value creation has to be flexible and adaptable. Like your strategy, it too has to evolve over time, and respond to—or better yet, anticipate—changes in the business environment or within the firm itself that can make its elements obsolete.

Philosopher Martha Nussbaum describes the balance in a system as a "fragile integrity." It is "impossible to build water-tight ships that will withstand all contingencies," she wrote. "You cannot remove ungoverned chance from human life."[10] And it is wrong to try.

As a strategist, you need to live with "ungoverned chance." Nussbaum talks about this as going from a "more confident to a less confident wisdom," cultivating "flexible responsiveness, rather than rigid hardness."[11] This requires letting go of a "rage for control" and being open to rethinking and refashioning elements of your strategy.

Even more fundamentally, as a leader you must allow yourself to be open to reinterpreting what your business is about. Just as it is necessary to stake out a purpose, a leader must be open to rethinking that purpose in order to move the business forward. Theseus was willing to change over every part of his ship to preserve its seaworthiness. As a strategist, you must be willing to replace virtually every component of your business to extend its relevance and future.

There is a temptation, I think widespread, to believe that the firm comprises its parts and their alignment, and that certain parts of the business are so critical to what a firm is that without them the firm, in an important sense, ceases to be. You are the one who must resist this temptation and persuade others when big changes are due. Pablo Picasso put it bluntly: "Success is dangerous. One begins to copy oneself, and to copy oneself is more dangerous than to copy others. It leads to sterility."[12]

Very rare is the leader who will not, at some point in his or her career, have to overhaul a company's strategy in perhaps dramatic ways. Sometimes this brings moments of epiphany—eureka flashes of insight that ignite dazzling new ways of thinking about an enterprise, its purpose, its potential. I have witnessed some of these moments, in small group meetings or even in the classroom, as managers reconceptualize what their organizations do and are capable of doing. These episodes are inspiring. They can become catalytic.

Other times these decisions can be wrenching, particularly if you have built a business that may need to be taken apart and put back together again in a new way. More than one owner or manager—men and women coming to grips with what their organizations are and what they want them to become—has described that retooling as an intense personal struggle. Recall real estate entrepreneur Kerr Taylor's anguished decision in chapter 6 to shut down his original broker-dealer business in the economic downturn. Though it no longer offered his company a strategic advantage, he was emotionally attached to it and couldn't let go. When he finally faced up to reality and closed it, he said, "It was one of the hardest things I ever did."

Yet those same people often say that the experience was one of the most rewarding of their lives. It can be profoundly liberating as a kind of corporate rebirth or creation. An executive student, the CEO of a large Asian firm, once described his own experience: "I love our business, our people, the challenges, the fact that other people get deep benefits from what we sell," he said. "Even so, in the coming years, I can see that we will need to go in a new direction, and that will mean selling off parts of the business. The market has gotten too competitive, and we don't make the margins we used to." He winced as he admitted this.

Then he lowered his voice and added something surprising. "At a fundamental level, though, it's changes like this that keep us fresh, and keep me going. While it can be painful when it happens, in the long run I wouldn't want to lead a company that didn't reinvent itself."

Done well, undertaken organically, the exercise of crafting strategy becomes a journey that can renew both a company and a leader. Those who shoulder the responsibilities of an owner or top manager likely already know the satisfaction of building something, creating something that would not have otherwise existed. Max De Pree, the legendary CEO of Herman Miller, said it well: "In the end, it is important to remember that we cannot become what we need to be by remaining what we are."[13]

And that, finally, is the point of everything, isn't it? Making something and helping it find its way. Continually refining and renewing its reason to exist. It is the enduring job of a leader. As we saw in Apple, businesses, no less than people, have to reinvent themselves.

GET YOUR TEAM ON BOARD

Even as you strive for a big-picture view of your business, you need to become intimate with it at the ground level. After all, you're leading a group effort. You need to connect with people throughout the business so that you can both inspire them and learn from them. If you don't fill them in on your thinking, they're not likely to make strategy part of their agenda. And if you don't enlist their knowledge in creating plans, you are wasting an invaluable resource: As the people who talk with the customers and do a lion's share of the work, they possess information you can't do without.

Thomas Saporito, chairman of RHR International, a management development firm, believes that many leaders get so locked into their own vision that they resist hearing when others don't believe in it. One executive he coached, a CEO of a Fortune 100 company, set ambitious goals but focused more on the soundness of his strategy than on others' acceptance of it: He "was so blind to how the board and employees really felt about it, that he couldn't gauge their low levels of buy-in." He was eventually asked to step aside. "Almost every CEO I've worked with stumbles at some point because of this," Saporito wrote. "When that happens, I remind them that executives don't get paid to be right. They get paid to be effective."[14]

Max De Pree was eloquent on this subject as well. He believed that everyone in an organization has a right to understand strategy and a right to be involved in it. "Good communication is not simply sending and receiving. Nor is good communication simply an exchange of data," he wrote. "The best communication *forces* you to listen."[15] Throughout, however, De Pree recognized that leaders have an obligation to provide and maintain momentum: "It is the feeling among a group of people that their lives and their work are intertwined and moving toward a recognizable and legitimate goal." Such momentum comes from a "clear vision of what the corporation ought to be, from a well-thought out strategy to achieve that vision, and from carefully conceived and communicated directions and plans that enable everyone to participate and be publicly accountable in achieving those plans."[16]

Napoleon put it this way: "Define reality, give hope."

That great advice acknowledges the importance of facing and interpreting hard-nosed economic reality (as Manoogian of Masco did not), underscores the need for a purpose and a plan (as we saw in IKEA and Gucci), and recognizes the *human* need of team members to be motivated and assured. In rallying the Gucci troops around his new purpose,

De Sole made it his job to keep people informed, while also responding to the rapid business changes around him.

"I was very good at motivating and communicating with people. I used to give speeches in the cafeteria so that everyone would know what we were doing," he said in an interview. "I was very decisive in upgrading personnel and making very hard decisions. I was disciplined, and under real pressure to perform. It was a constant process of making changes."

The hard and the soft, all in one.

Taylor of AmREIT speaks with enthusiasm about working on strategy with his team. "It starts with a deep dive," he says, "but then continues as an ongoing strategic conversation. Discussion is honest, open—which is particularly important when issues are tough." It took time and effort to reach this point, he adds. "Over the last ten years we have had to let go of a lot of ego and power levels." Now the team has a common language around strategy. Today, it's the glue: "We have conversations that relate to strategy in some way every week."

If a leader shortchanges questions of strategy, an organization and everyone in it will suffer. If a leader shortchanges the team and fails to clearly communicate that strategy, listen to others, or inspire them to get on board, the outcome will be equally bad. As a strategist, that means your ability to communicate—and to connect with others in the organization—is as vital to your success as anything else you do.

ONCE AGAIN: THE CHOICE IS YOURS

In the closing session of the EOP program, I offer the executives some advice: "On the way home, if the person sitting next to you on the plane asks what you do, simply say: 'I'm a guardian of organizational purpose.'[17] After that, you won't need to worry about any more questions coming from that direction!"

The EOPers always laugh, but by this time in the course, it's a knowing laugh. They recognize there's a real truth buried in the humor:

If they don't embrace the role behind those words, something essential in their businesses will be missing.

Working with thousands of leaders, I've seen that you don't have to be Steve Jobs to feel good about the contribution you've made, or the business you've helped to build. In my classes, it's not just the multibillion-dollar steel and world-class microfinance companies that bring satisfaction, but the candle company that began in a kitchen and grew to support not only the couple who started it, but more than one thousand others; the coffee roaster who stepped out of his family's business to offer a new value proposition to a new set of customers; the medical supply company that's grown with a family over three generations, each leader weathering his or her own share of crises and the ongoing need to find new footing, a new reason to matter.

Part of the gratification these leaders experience stems from grappling with one's business issues at unexpected depth, and seeing them in a larger context, such as an executive in a storage business who came to a much more sophisticated understanding of the impact of the powerful economic forces in his industry, or the owner of a financial services network who rebuilt his franchise from the ground up to serve a larger but less wealthy client group. Whether refining a business's purpose or direction, or how all of that is brought to life, leaders say they are grappling with their firm's future at a more basic level than they had before.

When pressed, some refer to the transition from understanding the broad outlines of a leader's role to a more grounded sense of what the position demands. Others refer to a newfound belief in the possibility of shaping their firm's future in a way that they had not previously considered.

A few individuals mention something else. Before, they say, they thought about strategy as a set of problems to be solved—the way it is so often approached in both practice and in school. Now, however, they're thinking about strategy as a way of life for themselves as a leader, a set of questions to be lived.[18] Miguel Aguiluz, the founder of Ink for

Less, talks about how he has internalized the process. He wants his businesses to be distinct, not only when they're founded, but over time. "I just find ways and means to be different from the other guys. That's what I do," he said. When working a new idea all the way through a strategy, he sometimes finds himself at loggerheads with his operations executives, who are reluctant to switch gears or change a good thing. But, he says, "an internally consistent strategy most of the time makes a winning company."

Each of these leaders invested the best of themselves in their work. They identified compelling purposes, built organizations to achieve them, and ultimately produced differences that really mattered. In doing so, they gave meaning to their businesses and also to themselves.

During the last days of the EOP program, I ask the class to read a rather unusual article by the late Harvard philosophy professor Robert Nozick.[19] It proposes that we substitute the difficulties and potential dreariness of daily living with an Experience Machine, a kind of virtual reality contraption. Nozick asks us to contemplate a world where we can achieve anything we wish, fully formed, simply by programming and stepping into this machine. With the experience prepared for us, there are no decisions or actions required other than choosing the experience itself. That means no sleepless nights, no hand-wringing, no agonizing choices or decisions. Simply step in and go.

As appealing as this may seem at first, few are tempted to accept the offer. They recognize that such pretend reality would deprive them of participating in the very actions that create the experiences. While the process of getting from here to there is not always enjoyable, and the end is not always favorable, the undertaking itself is theirs, it's part of who they are. "Should it be surprising that what we are is important to us?" asks Nozick. "Why should we be concerned only with how our time is filled, but not with what we are?"[20]

Reflecting on their own lives, EOPers often say that they like the accountability for their journeys, and their *uniqueness*. They like the "off-road," serendipitous experiences that would be missed in a preprogrammed existence. Imagine if Ingvar Kamprad had missed the boycott of his goods and the Polish solution that led to a completely new way to compete. Or if Domenico De Sole had continued to pursue his Washington law career and not gotten drawn into the troubled business of a client. Sure, these experiences could be dialed in, but first someone else would have to imagine them, and even so, the experiences would not be authentic, the rewards of lives that were actively lived.[21]

Nozick's Experience Machine is a fantasy, of course—at least so far—but it opens a door to thinking deeply about the meaning of what you do. How many people have you met who plow through life without a sense of purpose, who go through the motions, ape the ways of others, and get their rewards from keeping score? They may be highly accomplished, but there's little authentic about them. Sartre captured it with his challenging assertion: "Everything has been figured out, except how to live." The poet T. S. Eliot had another angle: "We had the experience, but we missed the meaning."

In 2002, Tony Deifell, a photographer and graduating MBA, zeroed in on this question. He asked some of his classmates to respond to a question in a poem by American author Mary Oliver: "Tell me, what is it you plan to do with your one wild and precious life?" Their responses, along with their photographs, became the basis for the Harvard Business School "Portrait Project," a tradition that has continued every year since.

At the close of my EOP course, I share Oliver's poem with the class, and urge them to visit the Portrait Project. While the exhibition is focused on people starting out in their lives, I believe it's equally important that we keep asking Oliver's question of ourselves, in our thirties, our fifties, our seventies.

In raising Oliver's question, the last thing I would want to do is "lead the witness" or attempt to equate being a strategist as the central answer to the query. But, if you're like the EOPers who respond with deep emotion to the poem, I suspect that many of you will find the connection. It has to do with the kind of contribution you want to make.

THE SUMMER DAY

Who made the world?
Who made the swan, and the black bear?
Who made the grasshopper?
This grasshopper, I mean—
the one who has flung herself out of the grass,
the one who is eating sugar out of my hand,
who is moving her jaws back and forth instead of up and down—
who is gazing around with her enormous and complicated eyes.
Now she lifts her pale forearms and thoroughly washes her face.
Now she snaps her wings open, and floats away.
I don't know exactly what a prayer is.
I do know how to pay attention, how to fall down
into the grass, how to kneel in the grass,
how to be idle and blessed, how to stroll through the fields,
which is what I have been doing all day.
Tell me, what else should I have done?
Doesn't everything die at last, and too soon?
Tell me, what is it you plan to do
With your one wild and precious life?

—Mary Oliver
New and Selected Poems (Boston: Beacon Press, 1992)
(Copyright 1992 by Mary Oliver. Reproduced with Permission.)

WITH AND WITHOUT YOU

You, like the business leaders and MBAs I have taught for more than thirty years, must ask not just "What would the world be like without my business?" but also "What would my business be like without a strategist?"[22] What if no one in your firm stepped up to the role? No one weighed the options and chose what the business would be—why and to whom it would matter? What if no one built a system of advantage that enabled it to do something in particular, particularly well? What if no one scanned the horizon with vigilant eyes, watched over the firm, kept it vibrant, and moved it forward?

I know these companies. You do, too. They're all over the world.

They're the lackluster businesses that seem to be waiting for something to happen. They're the down-on-their-heels ones, where people are working feverishly, but not making headway. They're the ones plodding forward, but never catching or creating a wave. They're the ones that don't cohere, or that work against themselves, undermining in one part of the business what they're doing in another part.

They're not the kind of companies most of us would be eager to work for, or, for that matter, to do business with. They aren't the companies making a difference.

By contrast, most of the business leaders I have worked with come to embrace the role of the strategist seriously and with enthusiasm. They like the inspiration they feel about what they do and why that matters. They like the feeling that the world with and without them at the helm would be different.

As a leader, if you ignore or underestimate your crucial, ongoing role as a strategist, something essential in your business will be missing. Answered well over a lifetime, the questions at the heart of strategy will help a company prevail. Answered poorly, or not at all, they leave it adrift and vulnerable.

Articulating and tending to a living strategy is a human endeavor in the deepest sense of the term. Keeping all the parts of a company in balance while moving an enterprise forward is extraordinarily difficult. Even when they have substantial talent and a deep appreciation for the job, some leaders ultimately don't get it right. Their legacies serve as sobering reminders of the complexities and responsibilities of stewardship. On the other hand, it is exactly these challenges that make the triumphs so rewarding.

AUTHOR'S NOTE

The examples and stories in this book are based largely on five years' teaching in one of the comprehensive executive programs at Harvard Business School. In the pages of this book, I refer to this program as the Entrepreneurs, Owners, Presidents program (EOP), though the actual name of the program is different. You can find more information about various executive programs the school offers at www.exed.hbs.edu.

In some cases, companies' locations or certain details about them or individuals have been changed or composites of student experiences have been created so as not to violate the privacy of former students. Where names of companies or individuals are disclosed, it is done with express permission, and the details in the accompanying discussions have been approved for release by the firms.

In some instances, I have presented cases in class in a different way than they are described here or used other cases than the ones in this book to make the same important points.

I run a nonprofit. How relevant, really, are these ideas for me?

A great strategy is valuable to any organization. At its heart, the goal is to give an organization a *difference that matters*, and enable it to do something of importance particularly well. Having a strategy to do this is every bit as important for a nonprofit as for a for-profit business venture.

It would be a huge mistake to think that nonprofits are exempt from the rigors of competition or to assume that how they perform and what they add won't constantly be evaluated relative to alternatives. To the contrary! Competition in the non-profit sphere is as intense as any, and most nonprofits operate on even tighter budgets, with scarcer resources and more diffuse pathways between them, their clients, and those who fund their activities. This makes the need for clarity and effectiveness all that much greater.

As a nonprofit, you need to have a good understanding of your purpose—what you will do and what you won't do—and you must build an organization that is parsimonious and tightly tailored to that end. That means you'll also need the metrics one would demand of any first-class organization. All of this becomes part of who you are: Hone it carefully. Doing so will not only make your organization stronger; it will also help you tell your story to all who need to know.

Is there still a place for SWOT analysis and if so, where?

We absolutely still need SWOT. It's one of those timeless tools that pull a lot of information together. It's a high-level summary of a firm as a player and of the competitive environment at the same time. It can provide valuable context as you refine your purpose and develop your strategy.

If you're not familiar with it, a SWOT analysis looks at a firm's own strengths and weaknesses, and the opportunities and threats in its environment, sometimes using a matrix like the one below.

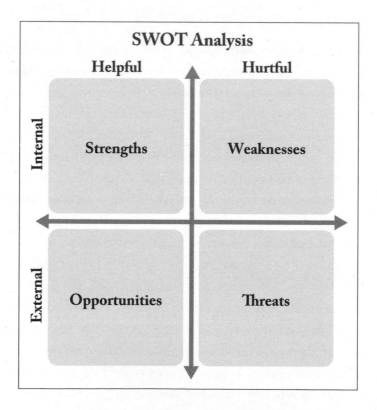

What's the difference between a vision, a mission, and a purpose. Do we need all of them?

A vision is what you want your business to be at some point in the future. It may be that you want to grow from a regional player to a national player, or from a national player to a global competitor. Or that you want to develop a service business alongside your product offerings. Whatever it may be, it is a picture of where you want to be down the road, and it's useful. A new CEO whom I work with was recently given this advice: "Start out with a picture of where you want to end."

Mission statements mean different things to different people and have been used in so many different ways that we've lost a clear sense of what they are or what they should be. Some are very broad, even lofty, and talk in vague terms about how a business will contribute to its community. Others are more narrow and closer to what I think of as a purpose, but often fail to connect with the real economics of a business.

To avoid this confusion, I use *purpose* to define why a firm will matter in its competitive context—the value it will add, and why that space will be different because it exists. That frees up *mission* to be used as it was originally intended—as a comment about the "higher" purposes of a firm and its relationships with society.

How do I go about analyzing my industry?

You can gain a lot of traction by starting with what you know. Gather a team and talk about each of the five forces in turn, drawing on your own experience in your industry. After identifying the facts, consider what they mean. Who has the power in this context? Why? Is it shifting? How? Overall, do the forces make the industry an attractive place to do business? Are some parts of the market less/more attractive than others? Are some players positioned worse/better than others? Could you be better positioned yourself?

There is a lot of relevant data outside your firm that can help you in this process: Government agencies and industry trade associations can be excellent sources for facts and statistics; prepackaged industry surveys produced by consulting firms or investment research services like Standard & Poor's often include detailed industry analyses, as do many analyst reports on key industry players.

A local public or university library should have access to publications and databases that can aid in your search, providing comparative data, market research and analyst reports, and recent newspaper and magazine articles. Factiva, Hoover's, LexisNexis, OneSource, Standard & Poor's, Thomson, and Business Source Complete, among others, provide various kinds of industry- and company-specific information and are available in many libraries or by subscription.

For an excellent discussion of these and other sources, see "Finding Information for Industry Analysis," by Jan W. Rivkin and Ann Cullen, Harvard Business Publishing, Note 708481, January 7, 2010.

To succeed, must I be a low-cost player?

No. There are many different ways to add value and many different ways to compete.

Historically, Michael Porter identified three generic strategies: low-cost producers; differentiators, who command premium prices for unique products; and focused firms who compete in very specific market segments, and could be either high- or low-cost producers. In practice there are an infinite number of strategies that are variations on these themes, and many successful strategies are not "pure plays." Nevertheless, the notion of generic strategies is a useful insight that forces one to think hard about how a firm is adding value, and the tradeoffs that may require.

In groups of executives, I've found that relatively few claim that their companies are low-cost producers who compete primarily on price. Recognizing that, a majority, and some almost by default, claim to be differentiators. They think of themselves in that vein, describe themselves in that vein, and some have the evidence to prove it. But a fair number paint alluring pictures and have everything lined up, except customers who appreciate their "unique" value and are willing to pay for it. To earn that you need to have a system of value creation that enables you to produce and market products or services with a true *difference that matters*. That generally leads to higher costs, but higher costs that get you and your customers something in return.

Many successful small and medium-size players focus on narrow, rather than wide, groups of customers, and make deliberate choices to tighten the scope of their businesses. This enables them to zero in on the idiosyncratic needs of a particular set of customers and build systems of value creation that meet those needs particularly well. Doing so can distinguish them from more generic players who compete more broadly, and make customers, whose idiosyncratic needs are now addressed, better off.

Many firms seem to get by without tightly linked systems of value creation. Why should I make it a priority for my business?

The intrinsic value of a well-developed system is perhaps easiest to see when a competitor tries to duplicate a successful firm. If you had the recipe, you could make Coca-Cola, for instance, but you wouldn't be able to duplicate its brand recognition, its supply and distribution lines, or its pricing. These are resources and activities the firm has honed over decades; the fact that they work together in a tightly linked system makes them all that much more difficult to imitate.

Years ago, some American investors tried to copy IKEA with a business called STØR. (Apparently the line through the O was supposed to hint at a Scandinavian connection.) STØR mimicked IKEA's look and products, but, after some initial success, it couldn't hold its own.[1]

STØR and other imitators failed because they could copy only single points of advantage. As Anders Dahlvig, IKEA's group president, said: "Many competitors could try to copy one or two of these things. The difficulty is when you try to create the totality of what we have. You might be able to copy our low prices, but you need our volumes and global sourcing presence. You have to be able to copy our Scandinavian design, which is not easy without a Scandinavian heritage. You have to be able to copy our distribution concept with the flat pack. And you have to be able to copy our interior competence—the way we set out our stores and catalogues."[2]

Success comes from a compelling purpose, tightly embedded in an interlocking system of value creation, and does so in a way that is difficult for others to imitate.

Should I try to develop a strategy alone or with my team?

Your team should definitely be part of the effort—but many leaders find it useful to first work alone through the strategy exercise outlined in chapter 6. You will likely find it a lot harder than you thought, and that experience will introduce you to the process and help you identify the issues that are likely to be most challenging in your company. Then, get your team involved.

Teams often begin by attempting to write out a strategy statement for a business. That's okay, but don't spend too much time on it at the start. It comes much easier once you've nailed the strategy. To do that, begin by developing an initial definition of your business's purpose (don't get hung up on words at this point) and work your way through a strategy wheel, spoke by spoke. This is an iterative process—refinements will come. As the big building blocks of what you do fall into place, revisit the purpose, and then come back to the wheel. As you close in on a purpose, and the activities and resources to support it, go back to the strategy statement. By then it will be clear what you need to convey.

How long should we expect to spend on the process?

Several meetings over a two- to three-month window should
be sufficient. If you're missing pieces of information, give people the
responsibility to locate them and bring them to the next meeting. It's
important to keep up the momentum and move toward conclusion.
Too many companies fall into a trap of "discussing and discussing
and discussing." In itself that could be a virtue, but strategy is about
choices. Reaching closure is important.

Should it be a democratic process?

Even with your team's help, as the head of the business you should
lead the effort. It is vital to hear others' views and get their input and
feedback, but if a clear and compelling direction doesn't naturally
emerge, you must make the call. Don't try to create a strategy by
committee. Relying on consensus can produce a less-than-ambitious
result and a strategy that is more like a compromise than an ambitious
aspiration.

That said, as we discussed in Chapter 8, it is important to keep in
mind from the start that you will need the commitment and support
of other managers and a wide swath of employees to execute a plan.
In his management development work, Thomas Saporito has seen too
many CEOs fail because they attempted to charge ahead without this
level of buy-in: "A CEO may be 100% correct with his or her strategy,
but without deep support for it from the board, senior team, and
employees, it doesn't matter," he wrote.[3]

Isn't it risky to put my strategy statement on my website?

This is a common question executives ask: Won't my competitors
find out what we're doing?

In reality, if who you are and what you do is clear to your

customers, it is also probably clear to your competitors. As with IKEA and Coca-Cola, if you're really good at what you do, there should be other barriers that will make imitation difficult.

The strategy wheel, with all its detail about your specific activities and resources, is an internal working document. But who you are as a player and why you matter should not be a secret; in fact, it is something you should broadcast. People outside the company as well as inside need to know what your business brings to the world and why it matters.

How often should we revisit the strategy?

In a relatively stable environment, big changes may not occur often, but the strategy should be formally revisited on a regular basis, once a year or so. This might result in minor course adjustments or a refashioning of some elements, often moving toward greater efficiency, and more effectiveness, in what you are already doing. In periods of more rapid change—whether generated internally or externally—these examinations may be less formal, occur more frequently, and lead to more significant change. In either scenario, to be worthwhile, these examinations should be fearless, thorough, and open discussions about exactly how your firm is faring in the marketplace and opportunities for improvement.

Beyond the formal processes, the leader of a business—the person who bears the most responsibility for its long-term health and vitality—should come to see everything that happens to a company through the lens of strategy: What do these events, activities, opportunities, or threats imply for us? What do they say about who we are and why we matter? How should we respond? This kind of engagement doesn't take place on a scheduled basis—it is ongoing and requires constant vigilance.

Want to learn more about the ideas and companies discussed in this book? Here are some of my favorite sources, with notes about why I've recommended them.

Industry Analysis

Competitive Strategy: Techniques for Analyzing Industries and Competitors, by Michael E. Porter. 1980; reprint, New York: Free Press, 1998.

This is Porter's classic work on industry analysis. It identifies five economic forces that influence industry profitability and have a great impact on industry-level profit. He talks about how to analyze these forces in your industry and how to position your firm vis-à-vis their impact.

"The Five Competitive Forces That Shape Strategy," by Michael E. Porter. *Harvard Business Review*, January 1, 2008.

This article is a short, straightforward presentation of the key ideas that are developed in more detail in *Competitive Strategy*. For a high-level survey of the topic, this is a good place to start. For a deeper dive, go to the book itself.

Strategy

"What is Strategy?" by Michael E. Porter. *Harvard Business Review*, November 1, 1996.

Porter discusses strategy as the creation of a unique position involving a distinct set of activities. It requires one to make trade-offs—to choose what to do and what not to do—and demands fits across all of a company's activities. Managers in my courses find the article both inspiring and practical.

"Creating Competitive Advantage," by Pankaj Ghemawat and Jan W. Rivkin. Harvard Business School Note, 9-798-062, Harvard Business School Publishing, 2006.

This nuts-and-bolts class note, originally written for MBA students, is a careful, straightforward presentation about several important strategy frameworks and how to use them in practice. Executive students have found its quantitative examples of added value and relative cost analysis particularly helpful.

Co-opetition, by Adam Brandenburger and Barry Nalebuff. New York: Currency/Doubleday, 1996.

This book shows how game theory can help a strategist think through a firm's interactions in a market. It moves beyond a zero-sum perspective on competition—where one firm's gains are another firm's losses—to a cooperative view, where firms create more value by working with, not against, customers, vendors, and others. It's an important contribution that could change your way of thinking about the goals and intentions of your strategy.

Blue Ocean Strategy: How to Create Uncontested Market Space and Make Competition Irrelevant, by W. Chan Kim and Renée Mauborgne. Boston: Harvard Business School Publishing, 2005.

Being different is one of the distinguishing features of a good strategy. But how to achieve that and, in particular, how to go about identifying the ways a firm might position itself apart from the masses is a challenge. Kim and Mauborgne make headway on this important question.

Creating Competitive Advantage: Creating and Sustaining Superior Performance, by Michael E. Porter. 1985; reprint, New York: Free Press, 1998.

This book is the companion to *Competitive Strategy* that focuses on industry-level analysis (see above). Here Porter zeros in on individual firms and how to create competitive advantage. Many managers find it heavy reading, but for those who want to dig deeply into competitive strategy, it has valuable insights.

Management and Leadership

Good to Great, Why Some Companies Make the Leap . . . and Others Don't, by Jim Collins. New York: HarperCollins, 2001.

I often poll business managers in class about their favorite business books. Hands down, *Good to Great* tops the list. When asked why they find it so special, they say they like the balance Collins finds between doing the right things strategically and getting the right people on the bus to do them.

Leadership Is an Art, by Max De Pree. New York: Currency/Doubleday, 2004.

De Pree writes with great confidence and wisdom about leading a company, and in particular about involving and inspiring people in the mission of a business.

Identifying Valuable Firm Resources

"Competing on Resources," by David J. Collis and Cynthia A. Montgomery. *Harvard Business Review*, July 1, 2008 (originally published in July–August 1995).

When managers try to identify the core competences in their firms, they often produce long, undifferentiated laundry lists. This article discusses what makes certain kinds of resources valuable, and why it is important to have such resources as part of your strategy.

Chasing Stars: The Myth of Talent and the Portability of Performance, by Boris Groysberg. Princeton, NJ: Princeton University Press, 2010.

Any manager who is tempted to blithely say that "people are our company's most valuable resource" should read this book. The research fully acknowledges the many contributions of individual performers but shows why that talent must be seen as part of a larger business system, not something separate from it.

Dealing with Technological Change

"Meeting the Challenge of Disruptive Change," by Clayton M. Christensen and Michael Overdorf. *Harvard Business Review*, March 1, 2000.

Christensen's research on disruptive technologies counts among the most influential management ideas of the last twenty-five years. This article is a good introduction to his work and includes references to his other articles and books.

IKEA

Leading by Design—The IKEA Story, by Bertil Torekull. New York: HarperBusiness, 1998.

This is the authoritative biography on Ingvar Kamprad, the founding of IKEA, and the philosophy behind the firm. It's a rather rough translation from Swedish, and hardly objective, but it gives a close-up view of the entrepreneur, often in his own words, and a lot of information about the role that purpose plays at IKEA. It includes the document "A Furniture Dealer's Testament," which lays out IKEA's guiding principles in detail.

Gucci

The House of Gucci: A Sensational Story of Murder, Madness, Glamour, and Greed, by Sara Gay Forden. New York: Perennial, 2001.

This is the story of a family business and a family saga so strange that it seems like fiction. Beyond its entertainment value, the book shows how easy it is for a firm to drift off course over several generations, and why family dynamics can add another layer of challenge to management.

Apple

Return to the Little Kingdom: Steve Jobs, the Creation of Apple, and How It Changed the World, by Michael Moritz. New York: Overlook Press, 2009.

There are many terrific books on Apple that cover various products or periods in the development of the firm. What I like about this one is that it gives an unvarnished look at Apple's earliest years—what it was really like—and what was working and what wasn't. A foreword puts that in context of more recent developments (Moritz's original book on Apple, *The Little Kingdom*, was published in 1984). Entrepreneurs who are starting out may find it inspiring to see how humble it all was at the start.

Steve Jobs's Stanford University commencement speech, June 14, 2005.

Text: news.stanford.edu/news/2005/june15/jobs-061505.htm.

Video: www.youtube.com/watch?v=D1R-jKKp3NA.

In this speech, titled "Live Before You Die," Jobs discusses some of the pivotal points in his life.

ENDNOTES

Introduction: What I Learned in Office Hours
1. This line of thinking was inspired by a discussion in *Co-opetition* by A.M. Brandenburger and B.J. Nalebuff (New York: Doubleday, 1996, p. 47).

Chapter 1: Strategy and Leadership
1. Ronald A. Heifetz and Marty Linsky, *Leadership on the Line* (Boston: Harvard Business School Press, 2002), pp. 53–54.

Chapter 2: Are You a Strategist?
1. This discussion draws from Michael E. Porter, Cynthia A. Montgomery, and Charles W. Moorman, "The Household Furniture Industry in 1986," "Masco Corp (A)," and "Masco Corp (B)," Harvard Business Publishing, Boston, 1989.
2. Besides faucets, Masco made plumbing fittings, bathtubs and whirlpools, builders' hardware, venting and ventilating equipment, insulation products, water pumps, weight-distributing hitches, winches, office furniture, brass giftware, and plasticware.
3. Porter, Montgomery, and Moorman, "The Household Furniture Industry in 1986," pp. 1, 5–6.

4. *Wall Street Transcript,* August 24, 1987.
5. Masco Annual Report, 2001.
6. Joseph Serwach, "Masco COO Follows Unit," *Crain's Detroit Business,* May 27, 1996, p. 3.

Chapter 3: The Myth of the Super-Manager

1. Richard Farson, *Management of the Absurd* (New York: Free Press, 1997), p. 15.
2. Jennifer Reingold, "The Masco Fiasco—The Masco Corp. Was Once One of America's Most Admired Companies; Not Anymore," *Financial World,* October 24, 1995.
3. "Mengel Company (A)," Harvard Business School, 1946.
4. Michael E. Porter, "Understanding Industry Structure," Harvard Business School course note N9-707-493, August 13, 2007.
5. This discussion of industry forces draws heavily on the seminal work of Michael E. Porter, including *Competitive Strategy* (New York: Free Press, 1998) and "The Five Competitive Forces That Shape Strategy," *Harvard Business Review,* January 1, 2008.
6. Large sample studies have found that industry effects across the economy on average account for between 10 and 19 percent of the variance in firm performance. In manufacturing industries, their effect is often around 10 percent; in some other sectors their impact is much higher. In wholesale/retail, lodging/entertainment, and services, industry accounts for over 40 percent of variance in firm profitability. In agriculture/mining and transportation, industry accounts for 39.50 percent and 29.35 percent, respectively, of variance. See A. M. McGahan and M. E. Porter, "How Much Does Industry Matter, Really?" *Strategic Management Journal,* Summer 1977, pp. 15–30.
7. This framework is due to Porter. See above.
8. Jack Welch, interviewed by Christopher Bartlett on December 16, 1999, Harvard Business School Media Services, Tape No. 10095.
9. Warren Buffett, Brainy Quote.com, accessed August 15, 2011.
10. W. Chan Kim and Renée Mauborgne, *Blue Ocean Strategy: How to Create Uncontested Market Space and Make the Competition Irrelevant* (Boston: Harvard Business School Publishing, 2005).
11. Reingold, "The Masco Fiasco."

Chapter 4: Begin with Purpose

1. "IKEA: How the Swedish Retailer Became a Global Cult Brand," *BusinessWeek*, November 14, 2005.

2. Bertil Torekull, *Leading by Design: The IKEA Story* (New York: HarperBusiness, 1999), p. 10. The book was originally published in Sweden as *Historien om IKEA* (The Story of IKEA) in 1998.

3. Torekull, *Leading by Design*, p. 10.

4. Ibid., p. 24.

5. Ibid., pp. 148–49.

6. Robert McKee, *Story* (New York: HarperCollins, 1997), pp. 181–207.

7. Torekull, *Leading by Design*, p. 50.

8. IKEA 2010 Annual Report.

9. Ellen Lewis, *Great IKEA!*, (UK: Marshall Cavendish, 2008) p. 39.

10. Ingvar Kamprad, "A Furniture Dealer's Testament," quoted in Torekull, *Leading by Design*, p. 228.

11. Ibid., pp. 228, 231.

12. These estimates are for 2004–2009 and come from "IKEA: Flat-pack Accounting," *The Economist*, May 13, 2006 (estimates net profit margin of nearly an 11 percent return for 2004); Kerry Capell, "IKEA: How the Swedish Retailer Became a Global Cult Brand," *BusinessWeek*, November 14, 2005 (estimates net profit margin of 9.6 percent for 2005, described by an analyst as "among the best in home furnishings"; "Ikea Forecasts 'Flat' Profits for 2010," *Local*, Swedish edition, February 22, 2010 (estimates net profit margin of 22.9 percent for 2009).

13. Rodd Wagner and James K. Harter, *The Elements of Great Managing* (Washington, DC: Gallup Press, 2006), p. 117.

14. Michael Porter makes a strong argument about the value of trade-offs in strategy. See "What Is Strategy?" *Harvard Business Review*, November 1, 1996 (also available as HBR Reprint 96608).

15. IKEA Vision Statement, quoted in Youngme Moon, "IKEA Invades America," Harvard Business School Publishing, September 14, 2004, p. 5.

16. These added-value charts were developed by the strategy teaching group at Harvard Business School and are based on the pioneering work of Adam Brandenburger, Barry Nalebuff, and Harborne Stuart. See A. M. Brandenburger and H. W. Stuart, "Value-Based Business Strategy," *Journal of Economics and Management Strategy* 5 (1996), pp. 5–24. Based

on a suggestion by Adam Brandenburger, and to create a parallel with
the line labeled "Willingness to Pay," I label the bottommost line on
the chart "Willingness to Supply" (not "Opportunity Cost," as in the
Brandenburger and Stuart article). These ideas are also developed in
A. M. Brandenburger and B. J. Nalebuff, *Co-opetition* (New York:
Doubleday, 1996).

17. Ibid.
18. Moon, "IKEA Invades America."
19. Pankaj Ghemawat and Jan W. Rivkin, "Creating Competitive
    Advantage," Harvard Business School course note 798-062, February
    25, 2006, p. 7.
20. This wonderful question arises from a discussion in Brandenburger and
    Nalebuff, *Co-opetition*, p. 47ff, where they discuss, among other things, the
    classic movie *It's a Wonderful Life* and ask "What is your added value?"

Chapter 5: Turn Purpose into Reality

1. I was first introduced to the Gucci story through David Yoffie's case on
   the company: "Gucci Group N.V. (A)," Harvard Business Publishing,
   Boston, May 10, 2001. He has since written a second case on the
   company, "Gucci Group in 2009," January 14, 2009.
2. Sara Gay Forden, *The House of Gucci* (New York: Perennial, 2001), p. 251.
3. The idea to illustrate Gucci's development over time in this way is drawn
   from David Yoffie's original teaching plan for the Gucci case.
4. In "What Is Strategy," *Harvard Business Review*, November–December
   1996, p. 62, Porter introduces the idea of a Productivity Frontier to
   identify firms in an industry that are best in class. A firm's particular
   location on the frontier identifies its positioning in the industry; if a
   firm is off the frontier it means either that its costs are too high or its
   nonprice-buyer value delivered is too low, relative to other players in the
   industry. The charts used in this chapter are inspired by Porter's work,
   but the titles and axes have been modified.
5. Forden, *The House of Gucci*, p. 119.
6. Luisa Zargani, "True Confessions," *Women's Wear Daily*, June 5, 2006,
   p. 30.
7. Forden, *The House of Gucci*, p. 63.
8. Ibid., p. 110.
9. Ibid., p. 155.

10. As quoted in David Yoffie, "Gucci Group N.V. (A)," Harvard Business Publishing, January 14, 2009, p. 3.
11. Forden, *The House of Gucci*, p. 142.
12. Yoffie, "Gucci Group N.V. (A)," p. 7.
13. Forden, *The House of Gucci*, p. 167.
14. It was soon the end of Maurizio, too. A year and a half later he was murdered by a hit man hired by his ex-wife.
15. Author's interview with De Sole, August 10, 2010.
16. Ibid.
17. Ibid.
18. Yoffie, "Gucci Group N.V. (A)," p. 9.
19. Ibid.
20. Forden, *The House of Gucci*, p. 255.
21. Ibid., p. 259.
22. Gucci.com, under Gucci history, 1990s.
23. Credit Suisse First Boston Equity Research, "Gucci Group N.V.," March 9, 2001, p. 3.
24. Lauren Goldstein, "Style Wars," *Time*, April 9, 2001.
25. Amy Barrett, "Fashion Model: Gucci Revival Sets Standard in Managing Trend-Heavy Sector: Italian House Buffs Brand by Focusing on Quality, Exclusivity and Image—Hidden Costs of Cachet?" *Wall Street Journal Europe*, August 25, 1997.
26. Forden, *The House of Gucci*, p. 185.
27. Ibid., p. 142.
28. Author's interview with De Sole, August 10, 2010.
29. Credit Suisse, "Gucci Group N.V.," p. 14.
30. Author's interview with De Sole, August 10, 2010.
31. Credit Suisse, "Gucci Group N.V.," p. 10.
32. Author's interview with De Sole, August 10, 2010.
33. Ibid.
34. Yoffie, "Gucci Group N.V. (A)," p. 8.
35. Author's interview with De Sole, August 10, 2010.
36. Porter, "What Is Strategy?"
37. Author's interview with De Sole, August 10, 2010.
38. Forden, *The House of Gucci*, pp. 322–24.
39. *Wall Street Journal*, March 6, 2003.
40. Author's interview with De Sole, August 10, 2010.

41. "The Turnaround Champ of Haute Couture," *Fortune*, November 12, 1997, pp. 305–6.

42. Porter makes this point persuasively in "What Is Strategy?"

Chapter 6: Own Your Strategy

1. The strategy exercise described here, in particular the section on developing a strategy statement, owes a great tribute to the work of my late colleague Michael G. Rukstad. A posthumous article describing that work, David G. Collis and Michael G. Rukstad's "Can You Say What Your Strategy Is?" was published in the *Harvard Business Review*, April 1, 2008. Michael and I worked together on the first iteration of the strategy exercise in EOP.

2. James Champy, "Three Ways to Define and Implement a Corporate Strategy," July 13, 2006, column accessed via Searchcio.com, August 31, 2011.

3. http://www.pg.com, accessed August 31, 2011.

4. http://www.nike.com, accessed September 22, 2007.

5. http://www.google.com, accessed September 22, 2007.

6. ttp://www.bmwgroup.com, accessed January 6, 2011.

7. Elzinga, Kenneth G. and David E. Mills, "Leegin and Precompetitive Resale Price Maintenance," *The Antitrust Bulletin* Volume 55, no. 2, summer 2010.

8. Ibid. *See also:* Stephen Labaton, "Century-Old Ban Lifted on Minimum Retail Pricing," *New York Times*, June 20, 2007.

9. http://www.FourSeasons.com, accessed September 22, 2007.

10. "About the Economist Group," http://www.Economist.com, accessed August 31, 2011.

11. http://www.Doctorswithoutborders.org, accessed July 12, 2011.

Chapter 7: Keep It Vibrant

1. David Yoffie has developed a series of excellent Apple cases over the years that allow executives to examine the company and the industry as it was at various points in time. See, for example, "Apple Inc in 2010," "Apple Computer, 2006," "Apple Computer in 2002," "Apple Computer 1995," and "Reshaping Apple's Destiny—1992," Harvard Business Publishing, Boston.

2. Michael Moritz, *Return to the Little Kingdom* (New York: Overlook Press, 2009), p. 183. In 1984 Moritz published his original history of Apple, *The Little Kingdom*.

3. Alan Deutschman, *The Second Coming of Steve Jobs* (New York: Broadway Books, 2000), p. 54.

4. Moritz, *Return to the Little Kingdom*, p. 194.

5. Ibid., pp. 217–18.

6. Ibid., p. 242.

7. Ibid., p. 257.

8. Ibid., p. 276.

9. Ibid., p. 206.

10. Ibid., p. 268.

11. Ibid., p. 304.

12. Jeffrey S. Young and William L. Simon, *iCon* (Hoboken, NJ: Wiley, 2005), p. 80.

13. Owen W. Linzmayer, *Apple Confidential 2.0* (San Francisco: No Starch Press, 2008), pp. 77–78.

14. Lee Butcher, *Accidental Millionaire: The Rise and Fall of Steve Jobs at Apple Computer* (New York: Knightsbridge, 1990), p. 174.

15. Young and Simon, *iCon*, p. 70.

16. Linzmayer, *Apple Confidential 2.0*, p. 154.

17. Moritz, *Return to the Little Kingdom*, p. 332.

18. Linzmayer, *Apple Confidential 2.0*, p. 157.

19. Ibid., p. 158.

20. http://Jeremyreimer.com/postman/node/329.

21. Linzmayer, *Apple Confidential 2.0*, p. 161.

22. Yoffie, "Apple Computer, 2006," p. 4.

23. Brent Schlender, "Something's Rotten in Cupertino," *Fortune*, March 3, 1997, p. 100.

24. Linzmayer, *Apple Confidential 2.0*, pp. 263–69.

25. Joseph A. Schumpeter, *Capitalism, Socialism and Democracy* (1943; reprinted, Taylor & Francis e-library, 2003), p. 84.

26. Bear Stearns, "Computer Hardware," Equity Research, July 2002.

27. Peter Rojas, "Why IBM Sold Its PC Business to Lenovo," *Engadget*, January 1, 2005.

28. Moritz, *Return to the Little Kingdom*, p. 299.

29. Ibid.

30. Quoted in Linzmayer, *Apple Confidential 2.0*, p. 247.
31. Ibid.
32. Deutschman, *The Second Coming of Steve Jobs*, pp. 54–55.
33. Linzmayer, *Apple Confidential 2.0*, p. 210.
34. Moritz, *Return to the Little Kingdom*, p. 14.
35. Quoted in Deutschman, *The Second Coming of Steve Jobs*, p. 183.
36. Quoted in Linzmayer, *Apple Confidential 2.0*, p. 212.
37. Adam Lashinsky, "The Decade of Steve," *Fortune*, November 23, 2009, p. 95.
38. Quoted in Linzmayer, *Apple Confidential 2.0*, p. 292.
39. Quoted in ibid., p. 289 (originally appeared in *Fortune*, February 19, 1996).
40. Quoted in ibid., p. 176.
41. Lashinsky, "The Decade of Steve," p. 95.
42. Deutschman, *The Second Coming of Steve Jobs*, p. 249.
43. Linzmayer, *Apple Confidential 2.0*, pp. 295–98.
44. Leander Kahney, *Inside Steve's Brain* (New York: Portfolio, 2008), pp. 185–88.
45. Quoted in Steven Levy, *The Perfect Thing* (New York: Simon & Schuster, 2007), p. 51.
46. Quoted in Lashinsky, "The Decade of Steve," p. 96. Original in *Time* magazine in early 2002.
47. "Ship of Theseus," *Wikipedia*, accessed August 19, 2011.
48. Levy, *The Perfect Thing*, pp. 73–74.
49. Ibid., p. 3.
50. Apple 10-K, filed October 27, 2010, p. 81.
51. Jared Newman, "Apple iCloud: What It Is, and What It Costs," Today at PC World blog, posted August 2, 2011.
52. NPD Group Inc., "Windows Phone 7 Off to a Slow Start in Fourth Quarter, as Android Smartphone Market-Share Lead Increases," press release, January 31, 2011.

Chapter 8: The Essential Strategist

1. Heike Bruch and Sumantra Ghoshal, *A Bias for Action: How Effective Managers Harness Their Willpower, Achieve Results, and Stop Wasting Time* (Boston: Harvard Business School Press, 2004).

2. Stephen R. Covey, *The Seven Habits of Highly Effective People*, New York: Fireside/Simon & Schuster, 1989.

3. Richard Swedberg, "Rebuilding Schumpeter's Theory of Entrepreneurship," Cornell University, March 6, 2007, p. 7.

4. Schumpeter, 1911, as quoted in ibid., p. 7.

5. Swedberg, "Rebuilding Schumpeter's Theory of Entrepreneurship," p. 8. These are Swedberg's words explaining and summarizing what Schumpeter had written.

6. Seymour Tilles, "How to Evaluate Corporate Strategy," *Harvard Business Review*, July–August, 1963.

7. Jean-Paul Sartre, "Existentialism and Humanism," *Basic Writings*, edited by Stephen Priest (Florence, KY: Routledge, 2001), p. 42.

8. Ibid., p. 29.

9. Helmuth von Moltke, quoted in *Clausewitz on Strategy: Inspiration and Insight from a Master Strategist*, edited by Tiha von Ghyczy et al. (New York: Wiley, 2001), p. 55.

10. Martha C. Nussbaum, *The Fragility of Goodness: Luck and Ethics in Greek Tragedy and Philosophy* (Cambridge: Cambridge University Press, 2001), p. 59.

11. Ibid., p. 80.

12. http://www.brainyquote.com.

13. Max De Pree, *Leadership Is an Art* (New York: Currency/Doubleday, 2004), p. 100.

14. Thomas J. Saporito, "Every CEO Needs an Executive Listener," Forbes Leadership Forum, July 21, 2011.

15. De Pree, *Leadership Is an Art*, p. 102.

16. De Pree, *Leadership Is an Art*, p. 18.

17. C. Roland Christensen, Kenneth R. Andrews, and Joseph L. Bower, in their textbook on general management, *Business Policy: Text and Cases* (Homewood, IL: R. D. Irwin, 1973), pp. 16–18, described one of the roles of the CEO as "architect of organizational purpose." I prefer the term "guardian of organizational purpose" because it encompasses both formulation and implementation, and because it implies a more ongoing responsibility.

18. This is reminiscent of the advice Rainer Maria Rilke gives in his classic *Letters to a Young Poet*.

19. Robert Nozick, "The Experience Machine," in *Anarchy, State, and Utopia* (New York: Basic Books, 1974), pp. 42–45.

20. Ibid.

21. David Baggett and Shawn Klein, *Harry Potter and Philosophy: If Aristotle Ran Hogwarts* (Chicago: Open Court, 2004), chapter 7, "The Experience Machine: To Plug In or Not to Plug In." This essay talks about an authentic life as one that is actively lived.

22. See final endnote in Chapter 4. The first question here—about what the world would be like without your business—is from Brandenburger and Nalebuff's book, *Co-opetition*.

Frequently Asked Questions

1. IKEA was so angered by what it saw as a deliberate attempt to imitate its look and products that it sued STØR, forcing the firm to change some operations. In time, STØR was unable to operate profitably and approached IKEA for help. IKEA acquired the firm in 1992.

2. Christopher Brown-Humes, "An Empire Built on a Flat-Pack," *FT.com*, November 23, 2003, p. 1.

3. Saporito, ibid., "Every CEO Needs an Executive Listener."

INDEX